MONOLOGUES AND SCENES

DISCARD

2011
THE BEST MEN'S STAGE
MONOLOGUES AND SCENES

Edited and with a Foreword
by Lawrence Harbison

MONOLOGUE AUDITION SERIES

SMITH AND KRAUS PUBLISHERS
177 LYME ROAD, HANOVER, NH 03755
EDITORIAL 603.643.6431 TO ORDER 877.668.8680
www.smithandkraus.com

A Smith and Kraus Book
Published by Smith and Kraus, Inc.
177 Lyme Road, Hanover, NH 03755
www.SmithandKraus.com

First Edition: March 2012
10 9 8 7 6 5 4 3 2 1

Manufactured in the United States of America
Cover design by Emily Kent, emilygkent@gmail.com
Book design by Nathan Spring, nespring@gmail.com

ISBN-13 978-1-57525-780-8 ISBN-10 1-57525-780-7 ISSN 2164-2346

CONTENTS

FORWORD IX

MONOLOGUES

ABSALOM, Zoe Kazan. 1
ALIVE AND WELL, Kenny Finkle. 3
BACHELORETTE, Leslye Headland 5
BARBARY FOX, Don Nigro. 6
BARBARY FOX, Don Nigro 8
BASS FOR PICASSO, Kate Moira Ryan. 10
BOTTOM OF THE WORLD, Lucy Thurber 11
A BRIGHT NEW BOISE, Samuel D. Hunter 12
CHING CHONG CHINAMAN, Lauren D. Yee 13
COLLAPSE, Allison Moore 14
COLLAPSE, Allison Moore 15
A CONFLUENCE OF DREAMING, Tammy Ryan 16
CRAZY HORSE AND THREE STARS, David Wiltse 18
THE DIVINE SISTER, Charles Busch 20
DUSK RINGS A BELL, Stephen Belber 21
EASTER MONDAY, Hal Corley 22
EXTINCTION, Gabe McKinley 24
A FELLOW OF INFINITE JEST, Don Nigro 25
GEOMETRY OF FIRE, Stephen Belber. 27
GOLDFISH, John Kolvenbach 28
GRAND CAYMAN, Don Nigro. 30
GRUESOME PLAYGROUND INJURIES, Rajiv Joseph 32
HELLO HERMAN, John Buffalo Mailer 33
IN GOD'S HAT, Richard Taylor. 34
THE IRISH CURSE, Martin Casella 36
THE IRISH CURSE, Martin Casella 39
THE IRISH CURSE, Martin Casella 41
THE IRISH CURSE, Martin Casella. 42
THE LANGUAGE ARCHIVE, Julia Cho 44

THE LANGUAGE ARCHIVE, Julia Cho 45
THE LANGUAGE OF TREES, Steven Levenson 46
LASCIVIOUS SOMETHING, Sheila Callaghan 48
LOCAL NOBODY, Nicole Pandolfo 50
THE LONG RED ROAD, Brett C. Leonard 51
THE LONG RED ROAD, Brett C. Leonard 53
THE LONG RED ROAD, Brett C. Leonard 55
LOVE TOWN, Michael Kaplan 56
MATTHEW AND THE PASTOR'S WIFE, Robert Askins. 57
MOTHERHOUSE, Victor Lodato 58
OFFICE HOURS, A. R. Gurney 59
OFFICE HOURS, A. R. Gurney 60
PIGMALION, Mark Dunn 63
THE RANT, Andrew Case 64
RANTOUL AND DIE, Mark Roberts 66
A RUSSIAN PLAY, Don Nigro 67
A RUSSIAN PLAY, Don Nigro 69
SEVEN MINUTES IN HEAVEN, Steven Levenson 71
STILL LIFE, Alexander Dinelaris 72
STILL LIFE, Alexander Dinelaris 73
THEY FLOAT UP, Jacqueline Reingold 74
THINGS OF DRY HOURS, Naomi Wallace. 76
THINGS OF DRY HOURS, Naomi Wallace. 77
TIGERS BE STILL, Kim Rosenstock 78
TIME STANDS STILL, Donald Margulies 79
TRUST, Paul Weitz 80
TRUST, Paul Weitz 81
THE TYRANNY OF CLARITY, Brian Dykstra. 82
THIS, Melissa James Gibson 84
WE ARE HERE, Tracy Thorne 86
WE ARE HERE, Tracy Thorne 87

SCENES

A BRIGHT NEW BOISE, Samuel D. Hunter 91
DARKPOOL, Don Nigro 95
DARKPOOL, Don Nigro 98

THE DEW POINT, Neena Beber 103

EXTINCTION, Gabe McKinley 108

GIZMO LOVE, John Kolvenbach 112

JAILBAIT, Deirdre O'Connor 115

THE LONG RED ROAD, Brett C. Leonard 121

THE MAN WHO ATE MICHAEL ROCKEFELLER, Jeff Cohen 126

OFFICE HOURS, A. R. Gurney 129

RADIO FREE EMERSON, Paul Grellong 135

RESERVOIR, Eric Henry Sanders 139

STILL LIFE, Alexander Dinelaris 143

TRUST, Paul Weitz 147

ZORRO X 2, Bernardo Solano 151

RIGHTS AND PERMISSIONS 154

FOREWORD

Here you will find a rich and varied selection of monologues and scenes from plays which were produced and/or published in the 2010-2011 theatrical season. Most are for younger performers (teens through 30s) but there are also some excellent pieces for women in their 40s and 50s, and even a few for older performers. Some are comic (laughs), some are dramatic (generally, no laughs). Some are rather short, some are rather long. All represent the best in contemporary playwriting.

Several of the monologues are by playwrights whose work may be familiar to you such as Don Nigro, Stephen Belber, Charles Busch, Donald Margulies and Naomi Wallace; others are by exciting up-and-comers such as Nicole Pandolfo, Leslye Headland, Tracey Thorne, Kim Rosenstock, Zoe Kazan, Samuel D. Hunter, Allison Moore, Lauren Yee and Steven Levenson The scenes are mostly by exciting new writers, such as Alexander Dinaris, Deirdre O'Connor and Molly Smith Metzler. All are representative of the best of contemporary writing for the stage.

Most of the plays from which these monologues have been culled have been published and, hence, are readily available either from the publisher/licensor or from a theatrical book store such as Drama Book Shop in New York. A few plays may not be published for a while, in which case contact the author or his agent to request a copy of the entire text of the play, which contains the monologue which suits your fancy. Information on publishers/rights holders may be found in the Rights & Permissions section in the back of this anthology.

Break a leg in that audition! Knock 'em dead in class!

Lawrence Harbison
Brooklyn, New York

MONOLOGUES

Absalom

Zoe Kazan

Dramatic
Cole, 41

Cole is something of an "adopted son" of a famous writer named Saul who took him in years ago and encouraged him to become a writer himself. Here, he reveals to the family that he actually wrote the novel for which Saul became famous.

COLE: Do you know what he was famous for when I met him? Finding new talent. That's all. In cer- tain circles he was known as a good editor with a good eye, who judged a short story contest at the Atlantic Monthly, which I entered and won. Of course, the contest was for college students, and since I was at the time trying to pass eighth grade at Allegheny Middle School, I had to forfeit the prize. But when Saul found out my age, and what I'd done, and that I, like him, had been orphaned ... he offered me a better prize. I could leave my shitty school and my foster home and Pittsburgh, and I could live with him in his beautiful house with his beautiful family, and he would help me become a writer. So I came. I lived with them. I wrote, we worked. My first book of short stories was a hit, the second one bigger. They adopted me. Member of the family. All I ever wanted.

And then, when I was, I expect, a little older than you ...
How old are you?

You must be older than you look. I was twenty-eight and I couldn't follow up. Overdue on my first novel, well bone-dry. Saul approaches me with a proposal. He wants to try his hand at this "writing" thing. He has an idea for a novel about an orphan boy who makes good. He even has a title: A Tender Currency. But he's nervous; he wants a partner. And he chooses ... me. Not Adam. Me. It would be our secret collaboration. Our surprise.

Have you ever been with someone where the sex was really bad?

If you like them enough, you keep thinking "It'll get better." And then it doesn't and the love starts to wear off, and you start to think "I could do better?" That's what reading Saul's first draft was like. I wanted so badly for it to be good. But it being ... so bad, it got me going. I put it all in there: my mother, my father. Things I hadn't thought about since

I left Pittsburgh. It was painful: Write what you know. After a couple polishes I sent Saul my draft. And that was it. Never saw it again. I thought maybe I'd hurt his feelings, straying so far from what he wrote. But he was kind, convivial Fatherly. *(A beat. Cole seems very far away.)* And the next thing I know Knopf is going to publish our novel. Except now it's his novel. He claims I gave it a read. He has my draft, I have no proof End of story.

Alive and Well

Kenny Finkle

Zachariah Clemenson, 30's

> *Zachariah is full time cab driver, on again/off again boyfriend to Regina,*
> *and part time Civil War re-enactor with an allergy to anything that smacks*
> *of being "farb" (his colloquialism for "fake garb"). He's been hired to guide*
> *Carla, an uptight NYC journalist, around the woods of Virginia looking*
> *for The Lonesome Soldier, who is believed to be a Confederate Soldier still*
> *at war. Near the end of the play with his annoying personality and tracking*
> *ineptitude having driven Carla to quit the search and abandon her article,*
> *Zach reveals the truth of the Lonesome Soldier mystery.*

ZACH: The Lonesome Soldier. I'm the Lonesome soldier, ok? You got me. Actually there are three of us. I got a couple of buddies - we trade off playing the Lonesome Soldier, one of 'em was supposed to show up for us sometime yesterday, another one on the first day but I suppose we missed them on account of the faulty compass and then the rain. I've been staging all these sightings all over the place for the past couple years to get people talking about him and to come down and look for him and maybe see him and maybe not because once they got down here I figure they wouldn't care about the Lonesome Soldier anymore because they'd experience this land the way I experience this land because I think this land is just the most beautiful thing on the entire earth! And it's got our history in it and we have to remember that! The land! To save the land! And I don't think we saved the land so we could pave over it and put a Target or Multiplex on it. I think we saved the land so that we can value it and cherish it and feel it. That's what you were supposed to be writing about. About the land! And Ms. Keenan, Appomattox! Appomattox is just the most beautiful piece of land. Just something to behold! And to think of what happened there! To stand there and know it happened right there, well that's just - that's just - I knew if nothing else that Appomattox would make you see! If you'd read the packet you'd know that. The packet is all about the land and the history for a reason. I've been trying to point you in the right direction but you're so damn stubborn and snooty about everything it's got to be your way or no way. But then last night you showed me this whole other side and I don't care if it was the whiskey that was talking, I like the way she was talking better.

I liked that whiskey tinged Carla Keenan last night and when you were up and singing that song I looked at you and something opened up in me and I feel kind of ridiculous saying it right now but for the record I gotta tell you - Ms. Keenan I think you're a 100% bona fide real deal not farb in the least authentic knockout. I shouldn't have done any of this. I see that now. But I couldn't help it. Regina, she kept telling me this was stupid. She thinks I'm a fool. Thinks that everything I believe in, is foolish, a waste of time. She thinks I should go work a regular job. That's what she says. Go get a regular job and give up this dream, let go of the land, stop re-enacting. But I couldn't help it, it's my passion. You know what I mean, don't you? You have a passion too. You know what it means to have a passion. Don't you? I know you do. Do you hate me? I don't blame you if do. Do you? You do. It's ok. I hate myself.

Bachelorette
Leslye Headland

Dramatic
Joe, 20s

Joe and a buddy have been invited to a bachelorette party. They don't know the bride-to-be; in fact, they don't know anyone there. They figure they stand a pretty good chance of getting lucky. Here, while the women are out of the room, Joe tells his pal the sad story of another buddy who came to a bad end.

JOE: I went out drinking one night with my friend, Ethan. We'd been friends since, like, 3rd grade. We got blasted. Stumbled back to my place and passed out in my bed. Lying side by side. He never woke up. He just never woke up. They said it was alcohol poisoning. But it turned out he had hepatitis too. So I don't know. He had started this whole heroin thing. Anyway… Maybe… there's something… he didn't look dead. You know? Even at the funeral, with the entire high school there, he just didn't look dead. It was like at any moment he was going to wake up and tell me I was a pussy for buying into this whole mourning and wearing black thing. I wanted to just get high. I felt like that was what he would've wanted. Not all this eulogizing and sober bullshit. But my parents… it was crappy. I had to pretend to be this person who was really concerned. That's not the right word. But I had to be this, like, adult or something. Why? You know? You can't just magically stop. Ethan fucking never woke up but it doesn't make me magically turn into someone who doesn't smoke or drink or get high or whatever. I resent that shit. Like the so-called "wake up" call. What the fuck? Ethan lucked out. When they put him in the ground, I knew he'd gotten away with it. He never… he never had to grow up. I know that's fucked up. But I feel like whatever… it's one of those nights right? I feel like you get it. Look at me. I'm 29 and the only difference between me then and now. The only change in 12 years is that I'm, like, taller. Not because I'm a loser. It's because I saw everyone scurrying off from that grave. Like "Holy Shit! We better all grow up. We better not end up like Ethan fucking Parsons." And why? For what?

Barbary Fox
Don Nigro

Seriocomic
Rem, 36

*Barbary Fox is a beautiful orphan, raised out at the dump by her strange
uncle Rem, who locks her in the fruit cellar every night to keep boys away
from her. She is very, very angry at him, and he is terrible at expressing his
emotions, but in his own grotesque and misguided way, he is trying to be kind
to her. Here he brings her her dead mother's old jewelry box as a gift. She is
very suspicious of him, and he knows he's botched
horribly any attempt to have a good relationship with her, but he's trying to
make her understand.*

REM: I brought you this. Jewelry box. It was your mother's. Thought you
might want it. Smells nice. Smells like your mother. Your mother always
smelled nice. Don't know what she washed her hair with. There's a onyx
pendant in there, some other things. Junk from the carnival Onyx makes
your dreams come true. Glad something does. Thought you might like it.
(Pause.)
Well, I'll just put it here.
(He sets the box down.)
I never did understand women. You never can tell what's going on
inside them. At least, I never had no luck at it. Buzzy Proctor, he brought
home a woman he met at the train station. I think she was unconscious
at the time. Or one of them was. She only ate seaweed, and spent all day
staring in a cracked old oval mirror. But when Buzzy got his arms blowed
off at the fireworks factory, that woman fed him apple sauce for seventeen
years, till he stepped on the cat and broke his neck on the porch. You
never can tell about a woman. Your mother. It was her and her sister, see?
Tootsie and Koralee. Two pretty girls. And I had, I just, I couldn't stop
thinking about her. Your mother. She was that kind of a girl, just stuck
in a man's head like chewed gum. Little bit of the devil in her. But your
father, my brother Franklin, he always had to have whatever I wanted.
That's just how he was. I don't think he could help it. I reckon it was his
glands. And he was a charmer, of sorts. Anyway, he got her. He got your
mother. So I married her little sister, Koralee. Don't know that I loved
her. Not then. But Koralee, she kind of grew on a person. Koralee was

kind of touched. She must have got it from your Great Aunt Fern, who used to talk to maple trees. Maybe you got it too. Sometimes I think you do. Koralee would get these premonitions. Sit straight up in bed all of a sudden in the middle of the night and say, The milk man's dead. And the funny thing was, sure enough, he was. Kicked between the eyes by his horse, when a hornet stung him on the ass. She had a gift. Anyway, I married Koralee, and after a while she kind of grew on me, sorta like a barnacle, and one day I woke up and looked at her sleeping there with her thumb in her mouth and realized I loved her so bad I couldn't stand it. And I just felt so damned ashamed. To have not loved her at first. And when your father saw I was gettin silly about my own wife, he tried to tell me them two boys of hers was his, not mine, and she was planning to run off and join the carnival just as soon as she got that baby out of her. I don't know if he was lying or not. With people, anything is possible. Then she died, birthing Dobbs, who had a huge damned head with nothing in it. Head the size of a pumpkin, and twice as dumb. Ugliest damned baby I ever seen in my life. Looked like he ought to be pickled in a bottle, shown at a freak show. That's when I really took to drink, serious. After she died. Probably would have killed myself with the drink except when your parents turned over the wagon I had to sober up in a hurry so I could take care of you two girls. Well, at least I stayed sober in the daytime. And at night I could always lock you in the fruit cellar. The way I kicked the urge was, I drank vinegar. I knew a man drank vinegar every day of his life, got some bad nuts, almost died of apoplexy, got over it, next day went to the zoo and had his head torn off by an escaped gorilla. Life is like that. I don't know. I just open my mouth and stuff falls out. There's your jewel box. If you want it. You don't want it, that's fine. Let me tell you something, Barbary. Never love anybody. You understand me? It's the single most important and only lesson I ever learned from all my checkered experience out here at the dump. Like people if you got to, but don't get attached, and never love anybody. Love'll kill you every time.

Barbary Fox
Don Nigro

Dramatic
Bert, 29

> *Barbary Fox is a beautiful orphan, raised at the dump by her strange uncle Rem, who locks her in the fruit cellar every night to keep the boys away from her. Bert is an occasionally charming but somewhat dangerous young man with a murky past who has appeared in town and possibly blackmailed his friend Silas into giving him a good job at the cheese factory and a nice house next door to his, and now he wants Barbary to marry him. She protests that they don't know each other and that people will think he's crazy to marry a girl from the dump who everybody believes is the town slut. Here he deftly cuts his way through all her protests.*

BERT: Barbary, you're making this way too complicated. This is a very simple thing. Here's the deal Do you want out of the mess you're in, up here by the dump and the fireworks factory and the chicken plucking plant, or don't you? Because I've got a brand new house at 413 Armitage Avenue, right next to my good friend Silas Quiller's place, and a good job managing his cheese factory, and a lifetime pass to his gazebo, and I'm absolutely prepared to make you my lawfully wedded wife this very night, preacher and papers and everything, and you'll never have to go back to that fruit cellar again. Knowledge is highly over-rated. Nobody knows anybody. Why waste six months pretending to get to know each other when at the end of it we'll be more ignorant about who we are than we were to begin with? You marry me and thirty years from now we still won't know each other. We might as well enjoy ourselves before we're old and ugly. Well, before you're old and ugly. I'm already ugly. But I'm not as old as I will be next week. So let's get married tonight, before I get older and you get ugly. You can see what a romantic kind of a guy I am, so what do you say? People don't think much of me now. I don't give a rat's ass what people think. I don't actually like people much. Most of them are stupid and the rest are evil or crazy, and a surprising number of them are all three at the same time. Just figure out what you want, then do whatever you got to do to get it, then grab onto it and don't let go. That's all there is. Anybody says different is a liar or a fool or both. Anybody don't like it, screw em. Now, you want to marry me or not? What's the matter? You want to get out of that place, I give you what you want, and you're too scared to take it? You want to spend the rest of your life getting locked up in the fruit cellar? Is that how it is? You like that fruit cellar? You feel safe there? Because let me tell you, sweetheart. Nothing is safe. No place, no person, nothing. And there ain't no cuddles in the grave. You want to be alive for a while before God kills you, or what?

Bass for Picasso

Kate Moira Ryan

Dramatic
Kev, about 40

> *Kev, New York City playwright whose career has seen brighter days, tries to convince his best friend and fellow playwright, Bricka, to bless a production of his new play, which takes as its subject deeply personal stories from Bricka's real life that could have a devastating impact on her and her son.*

KEV: Bricka, I live in a box, my job is pathetic. I want to have something to show for my twenty years in theater other than a box of clips and a GLAAD AWARD.I feel like I went to sleep at 28 and woke up at forty. I'm no longer the bright young thing. I'm no longer the engine that drives culture. I'm irrelevant. I want to be relevant again.

> *(Pause.)*

Bricka, I just want something for myself. Is that so wrong? I just want a hit. You wanted something for yourself. You wanted a girlfriend and a child and you got both. I feel as though I am suffocating from failure. Do you understand that? Can you understand that? I am in the same apartment, the same life, the same low rent job that I had when I was 25. I want to be someone. I want to have furniture that I do not find on the street. I've got nothing going on besides this play, Bricka. That's it.

Bottom of the World
Lucy Thurber

Dramatic
Eli, 20s

In a verbal montage at the end of the play, the characters relate their final fates. Eli describes his death in a mine collapse to his best friend, Josh, and explains the impact of being the survivor of the close-knit pair.

ELY: Inside the ground it is hot and cold at the same time. I eat in the dark. I shit in the dark. Arms, hands, legs and faces move and brush past me. A touch means a lot in the dark. A touch lets you know you're still human. This is gonna be hard for you Josh. It's gonna be hard when the mine collapses on me crushing me into the ground. You will sit in the room with my body. My blood will still be warm. You will touch my hand, my foot, my face. You will touch me until I am cold. And I won't look like myself. My life will be gone. You will know I'm gone. Not crushed under ground. Not snatched from the sky. But gone. Just gone. All the stuff that gets left behind. Do you sit with all my stuff? Can you still smell me on my clothes? Do you wake in the morning and forget for a minute? What makes you remember? Does your brain get caught on it? The fact of me. Am I still a fact? Am I more a fact than the loss of me? You'll sit down to take a shit. How magnificent to shit. A shit, enjoyable to get that mess out of you. You'll think about how, you never thought about shitting before. And you'll think about how I'll never shit again. Then you won't be able to help yourself you'll think-You'll wonder was I frightened. How long was I frightened? Did I know I was going to die? Does anyone ever believe they are going to die? It'll be hard for you Josh when you have to breathe. You won't be able to stop yourself because you are alive. Alive things breathe and every breath you take will remind you that I am not breathing. Until one day you breathe without thinking of me and then that will be worse.

A Bright New Boise
Samuel D. Hunter

Dramatic

> *Will, a disgraced evangelical who has let his own fundamentalist beliefs ruin his entire life, is presented with an option —hold on to his beliefs, or give them up and accompany his new love interest to a Lutheran service on Sunday. But when pushed, he clings to his former beliefs.*

WILL: Believe in what? Believe in the Lutheran Church, some branch of some branch of some branch of Christianity, some vapid, meaningless organization that's going to legislate my belief system instead of looking to God's word for it? You work at a Hobby Lobby, Anna. Before that you worked at Walmart, JC Penney, McDonald's, Barnes and Noble, and now we both work here. Your life is meaningless, my life is meaningless, and the only thing that gives any meaning, that brings any hope to this life is my unshakeable belief that God will come again in glory to replace this disgusting life with something new, and pure, and meaningful— And you could take the easy route, you could go to a liberal church, and believe in nothing, believe that God is unknowable and we'll never know the meaning of life, you'll go to college and get a degree in English or Philosophy or Art or Economics and you'll spend your life searching in the dark, trying to find meaning in meaninglessness— become one of those people who sit around in their fashionable clothes with their fashionable friends and call us bigots, and fanatics, and hicks, calling us idiots for actually believing in something, for standing for truth—(losing himself) AND THESE PEOPLE WILL BURN IN HELL, YOU WILL BURN IN HELL BECAUSE INSTEAD OF SEEKING TRUTH YOU MOCK IT, YOU INSULT IT, YOU SPIT IN THE FACE OF GOD AND HE WILL —

Ching Chong Chinaman

Lauren D. Yee

Seriocomic
Ed, 40s

Ed is instructing a house guest named J on the finer points of golf.

ED: Some people say golf is a white man's sport. I say, if you're gonna have that attitude, you might as well call America a white man'scountry. But look at all the Chinese Americans excelling athletically. Michelle Kwan. Yao Ming. Kristi Yamaguchi. Makes you think. Now, in the business world, golf is of the utmost importance. During those games, lives are changed. Men are made. The stakes are enormous. So when you play golf, you need to be aware. Of your grip. Of your stance. And every time you tee off, you want to ask yourself some questions. Such as:

Does my swing feel natural?

Do I commit with my follow-through?

What club should I be using?

Am I hitting it at the right spot?

Did I wash my balls today?

And most importantly: can I get it in the hole?

And the answer is: no. NEVER. And you can't just upgrade your equipment because it's the only club God gave you and sometimes I just want to say, "Shut up: keep your head down and spread your legs wider and maybe it'd go in for once!" (stops, then...) But that's just because you always want to aim for perfection. And practice your golf swing.

Collapse
Allison Moore

Ted, 50s
Comic

> *Ted, a Southern gentleman, has just busted Hannah for eavesdropping on his 12-step meeting in a church basement, which Hannah has assumed is an AA meeting. After revealing that she's looking for a support group for her husband and that her life is a wreck, Ted feels the need to correct Hannah's misperception about what kind of meeting he was holding, and offer her some support.*

TED: I'm not an alcoholic. This meeting that just let out here is an SAA meeting. Sex Addicts Anonymous. The meeting that was going on down the hall is a gambling meeting, I think, so I'm not too sure where your support group might be. Now upstairs, I know, is the women's Al-Anon group. Whether they're all lesbians or not, I cannot attest. But I go to Al-Anon from time to time, and it's a good program. From the little you've shared about your situation, you might find it very helpful. The name's Ted. You've got a lot on your plate, from the sound of it. Happens to the best of us. Why don't we get a cup of coffee, what do you think about that? There's a little place around the corner. There's nothing sexual in my offer. Not that you're not an attractive woman, you certainly are. And, well, now, this is the part where you say I'm an attractive man, and you're sorely disappointed that my intentions are pure. Just a little bit of humor there. Breaks the tension. You just seem like you could use somebody to talk to. Twelve step groups all pretty much operate on the same principles, and you already know I'm a sex addict, so anything you say, I certainly will not be one to cast stones. The diner's got pretty good coffee, decent pie. But, you know, if you want to go home to your drunk husband and crazy sister, that's your choice.

Collapse

Allison Moore

Dramatic
David, mid-30s

> *David is a survivor of the I-35W bridge collapse in Minneapolis, which has left him with crippling panic attacks. He has never talked to his high-achieving wife, Hannah, about what happened. After learning that Hannah has kissed another man and that their marriage is in trouble, he decides to tell her about what happened to him on the bridge.*

DAVID: When the bridge started to go, I thought the world was ending. I thought a meteor must have hit, or a bomb, it was so loud. I was in between this bread truck and this orange car a girl was driving. She was seventeen, maybe? One minute I'm driving, and the next minute I'm sliding. The whole world went sideways. And we stopped, and the bread truck was still there, it slid right into me. But the orange car was gone. A whole lane of cars, just gone. And then there was a loud crack, and I was falling. I hit the water, and the car filled up so fast. I couldn't get the windows down, I couldn't get the door open. I started breathing in the water, I felt my lungs filling up. And all I could think about was you and our daughter swimming around inside of you, like a fish, you breathing for her. I still don't know how I got out of the car. All I remember is kicking towards the light and my lungs burning, like my whole body was on fire. And I broke through the surface, and I looked around to see what was left of the skyline, what kind of world I had come back to. And it hadn't changed at all. There was no meteor, no bomb. It didn't make any sense to me. It still doesn't make any sense to me. There should have been a reason, some visible reason it fell. But I guess it just happens. Things collapse. Bridges. Companies. Marriages. I don't want you to leave me. I'm scared, Hannah. How do we keep from collapsing?

A Confluence of Dreaming

Tammy Ryan

Dramatic
Peter, 49

> *Peter, an accountant, is talking to his wife Carol who, unbeknownst to Peter, has been having cybersex with a stranger she met on the internet. Peter suspects something, but other than being aware of Carol's general unhappiness with her life, he is not sure what. At this moment he has returned from meeting with the City of Pittsburgh's tax assessor in an attempt to dispute the current tax assessment of his house.*

PETER: They think I'm a nutcase. They don't tell you while you're standing there. They listen, they ask stupid questions, they write down the incriminating things you say and then they argue with you, try to belittle you, make you realize you have NO POWER. He argued with me. I said we have a plain old dinky bathroom on the second floor, and a tiny room on the first floor, not even a powder room, a pantry, not even a broom closet. And then he asks me about the one in the basement. A stinky little hole in the ground nobody actually uses. It's called a Pittsburgh Toilet, I say, and he says, I know, you live in Pittsburgh, that's why I know you have one. So I tell him, Okay, in theory, I have three bathrooms and he writes something down on his little pad. Can we continue, he says, and I say Yes, please, let's talk about the grade you gave my house. An A-. How can you give a house an A-,I demand, that has a roof like that? And he says, I actually never saw your house. And I was like, Why am I talking to you if you're not the assessor who saw it? Then he tells me this long drawn out story about his brother in law who was out of work, and he filled in for him a couple of times when he had to go to a closing or something. And I have to understand family or maybe he said the economy and I was like, Look, can I talk to you mano to mano? I say, we actually have a lot in common. You over assessed my house, and I over assessed my marriage. I say, Of course a realtor stands to gain by inflating the market value of homes in his selling area, just as a husband stands to gain a good night's sleep by assuming he is happy in his domestic area, so we were on the same page finally. Although he was getting a little defensive, like you are, so I said, Hey, I am not accusing you of anything INTENTIONAL, only that you can see how you might tip things a teensy weensy bit in your favor, maybe subconsciously, without realizing what you were doing. So,

I got his attention now and I continue. Faced with the results, you can see where you made a mistake, and once you see this plain as day, you can make adjustments for reality. You can lower my property taxes and I can fix my roof. Do you get the metaphor, now, Carol?

Crazy Horse and Three Stars

David Wiltse

Dramatic
Crazy Horse, 30s

Crazy Horse, war chief of the Lakota Sioux, addresses General Crook who has defeated his people and consigned Crazy Horse to the reservation.

CRAZY HORSE: It is as you say: we are always in danger out there. But I am told you are the one who can stop the danger. I am told you know how the world must be, that we have struggled for our lifetimes and do not know what you know about how to avoid danger or how to get food or how to stay dry in a storm. I am told your knowledge is so vast that you must bethe one who makes the green pastures, who sends the rain, who commands the wind. For it is you who determines who may eat-and whether they deserve to have food at all. Prior to your coming, in our ignorance we ate when we were hungry and shared our food with all but you know better and you have said that only those who live on the agency may eat. It seems you are right for those with you are as fat as soldiers while my village has chewed their own moccasins in the winter and our skin hangs loose upon our bones. Since you are the one who controls the food I shall watch with awe as you bring f There are many men in the world who

There are many men in the world who are big chiefs and command many people, but Three Stars, I think, is the greatest of them all. You want to be our father and to instruct us as your children. This is good because we need instruction. We have done poorly on our own and squandered what we had, as children will. Once we held the land from the Missouri to the Bitterroot Mountains, from the Black Hills to the Platte, but we used it ill, you tell us. We used it only to house and feed our people, knowing not what else the land was for. Now it is ours no longer for you have seen that we misused it and have taken it from us for our own good, for you are a stern and caring father. You have provided us instead with the cage you call an agency and I am glad that you will be our father and teach us how to use it for I confess to you we do not understand how to make a living from this barren patch upon the noble expanse that once was ours. But as your children, you will raise us up and teach us .. Whenever a man raises anything, even a dog, he thinks well of it, and treats it well. I see around you many whom you have raised up and you treat them as wellas dogs. And they are grateful and lick your hand as they should for a master must be a master and a dog a dog.

The Divine Sister

Charles Busch

Comic
Jeremy, 30's-40's.

Jeremy is a virile, charming man of the world, wry and intelligent. He's speaking to a nun, Sister Acacius, who he knew years before she entered the convent.

JEREMY: Susan and I had a tremendous fight and like an idiot I took the first overseas assignment I could find. I spent years as a war correspondent. I see now that I was desperately trying to compete with the legend of my father. Big Jack Templeton; the greatest newspaper man of his day. I could never compete with him. I couldn't out drink him. I certainly couldn't out write him. I can tell you this but no one else. My father was also famous for the gargantuan size of his penis. Big Jack's notorious twelve inch sinker. Naturally, mine was one inch shorter. Thank you for listening. It means a lot. Yes, in Tokyo, I paraded my giant schlong in the public bath to intimidate the Japanese men with their small endowments. In Dublin, I hauled out my humongous dick at every urinal so those afflicted with the "Irish inch" could get a good jealous peek. I got my comeuppance when I was seduced into marrying the scandalous American heiress, Valerie Blair. It wasn't till our wedding night when I realized that my bride had purchased me for my celebrated sexual organ. Valerie was obsessed with every facet of my penis; the massive mushroom head and the long shaft that's thicker than a beer can. She liked nothing more than to feel the heavy weight of my low hanging testicles in the palm of her hand. She called them her plump beggar's purses. Gee, thanks again for being such a great listener.

Dusk Rings a Bell
Stephen Belber

Dramatic
Ray, 40

> *Ray is recounting the first time he met Molly, 24 years earlier, having not seen her since.*

RAY: I actually do remember her. It just takes a while, when you haven't thought of something in a lotta years. But the lifeguard chair thing helps. *(Pause.)* The girl with the syrup lips. Which I wouldn't have connected her to. Not to those lips...not with a hundred guesses. Even now as she's telling me. Not that she's not... It's just that you hold these things in your head, and maybe every ten years or so they re-surface: Kissing a girl with syrup lips, at the end of a long day, on a lifeguard stand. And you think, well man, isn't that just an over-romanticized little thing—that you're not even sure is real And then you move on. *(Beat.)* It's funny 'cause when I remember that day now, as she comes into focus, from out of this almost floating brain picture of syrup lips, I know that the reason it's just an image, and not a full memory, is because afterwards I got really ashamed. *(Pause.)*Because I thought I'd pissed her off. Because all the time we were kissing I was trying to stick my hands up her shirt. Which she wouldn't let me do. And so for a while I just squeezed her, I guess you would say, her half-formed breasts, from outside her shirt. And then I gave up on the breasts and tried to go down her pants, and she still wouldn't let me. I think I probably tried like 17 times to get inside her shorts while we were up there, but she was pretty firm against it. It was almost like, as much as I was enjoying the kissing, it wasn't gonna be enough. Like I needed more because … because that's what I thought I needed. *(Pause.)* And I remember thinking after, "God, she must've hated me for trying to get down her pants 17 times." I was totally embarrassed, even as I walked her home later. *(Pause.)* But then I thought, "Well I'm a guy, so I guess that's what we do. She understands." And I sorta let it go. *(Pause.)* I don't think I've even thought about that since it happened. Even though I sometimes remember the lips.

Easter Monday

Hal Corley

Dramatic
Billy, 20

The adopted son of an eccentric, overprotective, stay-at-home dad, Billy has contacted his birthmother, a Washington, DC secretary making a first trip to New York City. After a strained dinner with the timid, incurious woman, Billy's romanticized ideas about his identity are turned inside out. In a final showdown, Billy finds his father bragging to her about his son's biggest accomplishment — winning the annual "Bake-off" at age twelve. An alcohol-fueled Billy lashes out, indicting his dad's fanatical parenting style once and for all.

BILLY: No, you almost won the stupid Pillsbury contest. Not me. You musta' made up the ingredients one of those long days when I was at school. I'd come home, there'd be heaps a' dirty laundry, Mommy would wonder what you'd been doin' all day, besides listenin' to your Ma's old Doris Day records while you figured out which cereal box contest to enter. Or half painted the room another crayon color. She'd find stacks of coupons you'd, like, hoard, so you could wander round grocery stores.
   (Beat.)
   Y'know, people always did talk about you. Behind your back. It didn't start with the copy shop—Kids. Even teachers. 'Cause you wouldn't leave after ya dropped me off in the morning. You'd hang out, at first inside the school, till your loud voice started disturbin' people and the principal asked you to clear out. But even then, ya wouldn't go! You'd peer in our windows with that big stupid grin. Later on, you always got to school to pick me up like, forty minutes early. Rain, sleet, snow, you'd be out there, carrying my slicker and umbrella, chattering away to the Jamaican nannies about where to buy the kinda old-fashioned galoshes like they made when you were a kid. Every once in a while, coupla' other dads might show, too. Who took the day off. In shirts n' ties, carrying briefcases and fold-up computers. But the one dad who always had the day off didn't ever speak to them. You hung out with the babysitters. Used to bring them hot coffee or homemade lemonade in your rusty 1961 thermos. Or—somethng to eat!
   Your answer to everything, hot soup, loaf of bread from the oven.

But all that's just an excuse to finally get to some big old gooey treat. Then, remember? A "sur-priiiiiise," after dinner. "Daddy's got ya a surprise for after dinner!" Poor Mommy'd be locked in the bedroom, on the phone with, like, Tokyo. I'd be off taking my bath, still told I was too young to shower, right? Then I'd come in, there'd be some wrapped up thing, hidden. Something real useful when you're, like, thirteen. A stuffed Christmas elf with a note sayin' "Bet Billy's been a good boy this year!"

(Beat.)

That shelf fulla' junk up there? Most of it I got for After Supper Surprise, even when I was too old to want any of it. And whenever anything broke, you're the one who freaked … and fixed 'em with scotch tape or bandaids, to keep Mommy from throwin' 'em in the trash. Now you want to pack it up, move it to that house? For what? To open a junk store? Where you can sell the Good Old Days to a buncha "new friends" along the Navasink river? Gonna fill that big ol' empty Woolworths with all this useless crap? No, no, once we unpack in Red Bank, I'm gonna be buried alive in this!

Extinction
Gabe McKinley

Seriocomic
Max, 30s

> *Max and Finn, best friends since collage, take an annual vacation together, during which they ply themselves with booze, drugs and women; but this year things have changed. Here, Max explains his philosophy behind their debauched weekends.*

MAX: You know my philosophy... there's absolutely nothing honest about monogamy. Monogamy is about repressing every urge a person has... your complete nature. It is the essence of lying to oneself. *(Beat.)* I tell you man, it's in our blood... our particles...We are so fucking small. Don't you get it? We are fucking tiny insignificant blobs of banded together protein, sitting on some dirt in midst of a universe which is probably just a white hole piggy-backed on a black hole...My point is, asshole, my point is... don't try to deny yourself, because you can't. What are the two things that we as humans try over and over again to attain, but never can? Peace and monogamy. Fighting and fucking. Fighting and fucking. We can't help ourselves. It is who we are. *(Beat.)* Humans don't mate for life. It is a scientific fact. We tell ourselves we do, but it's a lie society forces on us... Because deep down - so far down - in the smallest darkest part of us - we know that if we do, we'll go extinct. Let the wolves and pandas that are too dumb to screw walk off into the species sunset. But not us... Our life force screams for us to protect and produce. It's bigger than us. Everything is bigger than us. Do you know what a sex addict is? A man. A fucking man. *(Beat.)* Every man in life - fathers, uncles, heroes and priests - every man in history...Ghandhi was a womanizer, Martin Luther King, even Christ hung out with a hooker - and it wasn't for the conversation...

A Fellow of Infinite Jest

Don Nigro

Seriocomic
Will Kempe, 45

Shakespeare is writing one night in London when his friend and fellow player Will Kempe, the most celebrated comedian of his time, becomes furious when informed that the company has voted that from now on Kempe will no longer be allowed to interject his improvised comic bits in the middle of the performances. From now on, they insist that he just speak the lines as written. For Kempe, this is a deep personal insult and a terrible betrayal by his closest friends, especially Shakespeare, who has been like a son to him.

KEMPE: Oh, the lines, the lines, the precious lines. You're so damned precious about your stupid damned words. Precious, precious, precious. Honey tongued Shakespeare. This ain't your damned stupid Venus and Adonis masturbational fancy ass poetry, Willy. This is the theatre. I'm an entertainer. We're entertainers. We're comedians. Comedians. We live by the seat of our pants. We make it up as we go along. The script is just a little road map. Something to blow our noses on and light our pipe with. The script is a jumping off point. That's all it is. You can take your damned votes and stick them up your wife's fat ass, you ungrateful, back-stabbing little sewer rat. I made you. I picked you up when you were nobody, a little shit-faced hayseed nobody, fornicating with sheep in Stratford. I gave you a job holding the horses, cleaning up horse shit, doing all the muck work. You were nobody. Without me you'd still be back there in fucking Stratford-Upon-Goat-Piss shoveling muck with your whore of a wife and your loony old bankrupt dad. I've had enough of you, with your precious script. Your precious words. You're so fucking precious about your words. This is not how we did it in the old days. In the old days we were making it up as we went along. And people loved it. It was exciting. It was reckless. It was alive. Anything could happen. The script is a damned straight jacket for a bunch of cowards too stupid to trust their own wits in the moment. Fuck the script. I don't need any goddamned fucking script and I don't need you. I don't need any of you.
(Building to a fine rage.)
Do you think I'm going to knuckle under to this sort of political bullshit? I don't need this damned company. I'll go out on my own. I'll dance my

way to fucking Scotland, farting Greensleeves as I go, and the people will follow me. Nobody will pay any attention to you. The theatre is not a building. The theatre is not a piece of paper with a bunch of chicken scratching on it. I am the theatre. Flesh, blood and gonads. You are just a bunch of fucking words. Precious, precious, precious bullshit. Four hundred years from now, they'll remember me, not you. Nobody will have heard of you. This will be the Age of Will Kempe. I am the theatre. You are nothing. You have always been nothing. You will always be nothing. Nothing. Nothing.

Geometry of Fire
Stephen Belber

Dramatic
Chuck, mid-50s

> *Chuck is a former army paratrooper-turned-holistic-speaker on the neurolinguistic lecture circuit. This is direct-address to the audience.*

CHUCK: When soldiers prepare for battle, they determine their geometry of fire. It's a strategy for defense; me support coordination measures; basically so they don't shoot each other. *(Pause.)* But the thing about these wars like the one in Iraq, like a war against any insurgency, is that they're fought on asymmetrical battlefields. Which is to say - as we all now know - they're not conventional war stenarlos, you're not fighting guys in "red coats" standing with their guns on the far side of a field. There's no logic to the whole thing, no predictability, no linearity. It basically just means they're coming at you from every which fucking way. *(Beat.)* Which is, of course, the point. About everything. Everywhere. In life. It comes at you. Life comes at you. You're standing in a newly paved parking lot on the banks of the glorious Euphrates river, smoking the day's last cigarette and thinking about the Michael Bay DVD you're gonna watch on your laptop that night. The stars are out, just like they've been over that river for a million years. and little do you know that some pissed-off Iraqi teenager's got you in his scope, the scope of the gun he took from the body of a Marine marksman he'd snuck up on and stabbed with a Steak knife. And this kid hates you 'cause of what you've done to his cousin and his country and his pride. And he's got you in his crosshairs on a glorious Iraqi night. It's an extremely intimate scenario. Exquisitely intimate. And what does one do to fight that? Is there a logic? A path home? A geometry of fire to defend against that cycle of death you're about to become a pan of, on this bizarrely asymmetrical battlefield? *(Beat.)* Well — if there is. it's to be found in our imagination. We have to use our will. Like that paralyzed fellow willing the computer cursor with nothing but the pure power of intention. *(Pause.)* We have to change consciousness, folks. We have to become willing participants in a profound transformation of human consciousness. *(Pause.)* Can we do it? Can we change the geometry within ... and in so doing, the geometry of the world? Well, the answer is yes.

Goldfish
John Kolvenbach

Dramatic
Albert, 19

Albert is talking to his father, Leo. Leo is a gambler and an addict. Albert went off to college and Leo was left alone. Leo has been dependent on Albert for all things for years. Leo gambled away all the tuition money and Albert was summoned home.

ALBERT: So the dean called me in. Could I come immediately. I thought something was wrong. I thought you might be dead. I walked across the quad. Thinking about did you get run over or something. Did you fall down. I felt sort of fine, except I could see little sparkles all at the edge of my vision, little lights. So I get there? His secretary brings me a cup of water. She has that look, you know, you poor kid. She's one of those ladies with a bosom, do you know that kind? She lets me into his office. I sit down. He's sort of a walrus. He asks me if I watch baseball. I tell him it's winter. There's silence for a while. He says, "Your pugnacious father called this morning." OK So you're alive. Then he tilts his head to the side. Something he learned somewhere. In the chapter on sympathy. "Your father informed the college that he won't be paying your tuition for the next semester." Oh. Did he. Ah-hah. *(Beat.)* I had an exam, I was up late studying, so I was a little dodgy anyway but I start to get a thing where the dean's mouth doesn't exactly sync up with his words. The sound is like a quarter-second behind. "I am not insensitive to hardship," he says. I am not insensitive to hardship. [Is there a way to make yourself seem like more of an asshole? Saying that? Could there be a bigger liar on the face of the earth? A guy who wouldn't know hardship if it sat on his face.] *(Beat.)* He says, "There is financial aid available." I tell him about your pension. He says how much. I tell him how much, "I understand," he says. You can see him doing the math in his head and see him thinking, like, who is this kid? Who let this kid in here? *(Beat.)* He says, "We have had cases where a family was touched by calamity." Were we touched by calamity, Leo? Is that what we were touched by? *(Beat.)* I told him, no, things were fine. He said you "concurred." Then he asked me how I would define "fine" and I said that if I had a baseball bat I would bash his fucking head in for him. I guess I didn't say that. He wished me good luck in my endeavors. He said that if my father had a change of heart we could apply next year, la-de-da. I said thank you and called him "sir" like it's 1954 and I walked out.

(Beat.)

I took the exam anyway. This afternoon. I just went and took it like nothing happened.

Grand Cayman

Don Nigro

Seriocomic
Leo, 60s

Leo is confronting two tough guys in a hotel room on the island of Grand Cayman, who have been hired by somebody to follow him. Leo is perhaps in his late sixties, once muscular, now gone to flab, face red and pock marked, large hands, wearing a baggy pair of swim trunks, an old Hawaiian shirt, flip flops, with strong, ugly legs and gnarled feet with revolting toenails. Half patrician, half gangster. He has told them a number of rather outlandish things about himself which may or may not be true, including that he was shot in the head by the CIA and has seven billion dollars in a bank account nearby. He has been, he suggests, a writer, a Broadway and movie producer, acquainted with all the popular icons of the twentieth century, involved with politics and crime, possibly insane, and just maybe the creator of the universe. He is loud, vulgar, insulting, angry, profane, but has a sense of humor about the bigger than life persona he presents. The person he refers to as Priscilla is a man named Murphy, who might be there to kill him.

LEO: Don't fuck with me, Priscilla. You have no idea who you're dealing with here. Do you know who killed Jack? You know who killed Bobby? Do you know Jimmy Hoffa is now the secret ingredient in somebody's meat sauce? I was sitting at the Sahara, watching Louie Prima and Keely Smith do "That Old Black Magic." Sam Butera was blowing on his horn like a whore on a rich man. It was a beautiful thing. And I leaned over and said to Johnny Roselli, I said to him, Listen here, butt face. If you guys go through with this thing, you'll never again see one cent of my money. I will not finance your shenanigans. I will not launder your shorts. Because I loved Jack Kennedy like a brother. Oh, I know, Jack had his faults, all of them with nice tits, but there hasn't been a man fit to lick his loafers since. It broke my heart when Marilyn died. She was a very smart girl, you know, but her heart was too big. She was crazy, like all the good ones. In the end, what can we do but kill them? We always murder our gods. Where the hell is room service? I ordered clams in 1947 and what did they bring me? Sheep balls. What the fuck am I supposed to do with sheep balls? We kill Jack Kennedy and then we elect a string of characters who are crooked as a corkscrew or dumber than a hot water bottle. And

I'll tell you another thing about this country: nobody knows how to fry an egg right any more. And eggs is the only thing left in the world that doesn't have fucking high fructose corn syrup in it. You want to know why your kids have got the intellectual capacity of a dog turd? Because they're about eighty percent high fructose corn syrup. Do you guys get what I'm saying here? So here we have a man with seven hundred novels to his credit, written in four thousand languages, a producer of major motion pictures who works every day with people with the emotional depth of a shot glass and the morals of hyenas, a man with seven billion dollars stashed in the Cayman Islands, money that every criminal in the world in and out of politics would give ten years of his life to get his grubby little shit-stained paws on, and I'm stuck in a room with no clams, two pussies and a whore who won't take her clothes off. This is the story of my life. Somebody is always shitting in my saxophone. Did you guys eat my sheep balls? Because if somebody ate my fucking sheep balls, I'm going to boil their dick like a Bavarian sausage. I once paid an accordion player a lot of money to castrate some Bulgarian son of a bitch waiter who spat in my apple fritters.

There is no point. There's never been a point. I got seven billion dollars in a tax free account in the Cayman Islands, and what the fuck am I going to do with it? Can it make my bowels work better? Do you know? Does anybody know? Nobody knows. Because there is no point. And I'll tell you what it is. How many whores can one old man buy? Did you ever read Tolstoy? Tolstoy says there is no point. There is no future. We suffer over the past, we worry about the future, but neither one of them exists. All that exists is here. Now. Right now. And her body. That girl's body. Right here. right now. Nothing else is real Everything they tell you in school is a bunch of fucking horse pucky. The United States of America is a mythological construction with the same reality content as the Easter Bunny. It doesn't exist. Never has. Money. Power. Violence. Corruption. Theft. Lies. That's what this country is made of. I know. I made it. I boinked Martha Washington in the rotunda.

Gruesome Playground Injuries

Rajiv Joseph

Dramatic
Doug, 30s

> *Doug, an exceedingly accident-prone man has loved Kayleen since he was a*
> *young boy. She is a very disturbed woman, and here Doug has come to visit*
> *her in a mental hospital to tell her the sad fate of their school, and to tell her*
> *that he has always loved her.*

DOUG: St. Margaret Mary's blew up. It exploded. It closed down like 10 years ago.

It was used by the diocese for storage. There was a leaking gas main. Kaboom.

So, I work in insurance now. I'm a claims adjuster. I got to go and investigate the wreckage. I go over and the place is collapsed. So I hoist myself up there and I'm walking on the roof and then I stepped through a weak board or something and this upright nail went clear through my foot. It was about 8 inches long. Then the board with the nail in it——that board snapped through another board and I broke my leg in three places. It took them 5 hours to get me out.

And then I got an infection.

And that's why I have this cane now.

But listen: I'm up there, you know? Stuck up there, waiting for them to come and get me.

And there were these severed heads of a bunch of saints that had ended up all over the place, and they were just staring at me.

And this owl was there too.

And so I lean over and grab the little guy.

I was in some serious pain, you know? And I just gripped him close to me, because...

Because all of a sudden, I was like, Where the fuck is Kayleen?

You know? All of a sudden, everything was clear... trapped up on that roof, impaled, surrounded by all the angels and saints...

That's my life, up there, Leenie. That's my life without you.

Hello Herman
John Buffalo Mailer

Dramatic
Herman Howards, 16

> *Herman is speaking to a journalist who is interviewing him on death row three days before he will be executed for the mass murder of 39 students and 4 adults.*

HERMAN: I shot her at an angle, so the bullet would go through her skull and blood would splatter all over Marsha. That bitch walked around those halls like she owned the place, And why? Because she was a nice-looking piece of ass? You think that's gonna fly in the new order?! Shit's going down, Lax. Being some sweet piece of ass or some hotshot reporter don't cut it anymore. It's the ones like me are going to run the show. Do you know what the largest generation is? Mine. We have more than the baby boomers. So, you can believe me when I tell you we're going to do a hell of a lot more than "Rock the Vote." More and more kids are going to realize that this is the only way to make you assholes finally pay attention to us. And when they do, watch out. I made damn sure to kill more people than that wackjob Cho. You know why? Because you have to reset the precedent. When Harris and Klebold lit up Columbine, the nation freaked out, But people didn't freak our when that kid brought a gun into his school in Georgia, back in June '99. TJ. Solomon was his name. You know why people didn't freak out? 'Cause he only wounded six students. He didn't even kill anybody. People looked at that incident and all they said was ''At least it's not as bad as Columbine." Not with me, Lax, I wasn't about to settle for some rinky-dink shit. Oh, no. I blew that dumb bitch's head off and made sure a little got on James Hankley as well. But I was never going to kill him, I wanted him to live, so he could write about the day in his precious paper. Marsha on the other hand, she didn't have a chance.

In God's Hat
Richard Taylor

Dramatic
Arthur, late 20s-30s

Arthur, a neo-Nazi skinhead, has just been released from a Federal penitentiary. He has shown up at a fleabag motel, unabashedly knocking on every door asking for a little travel money. Roy made the mistake of opening his door and now has to deal with a cunning and dangerous Arthur. In a bizarre twist of fate Roy's older brother, Mitch, just got released from the same prison. Mitch is a convicted child molester and survived a near deadly attack at the hands of Arthur inside prison. Arthur has no idea who Roy is or that Mitch has locked himself inside the motel bathroom. After pounding down a few of Roy's beers, Arthur is about to take to the road. He asks Roy for one last favor, can he use the bathroom. Roy denies him entry. A noise is heard coming from inside the bathroom. Roy and Arthur lock eyes. What Arthur doesn't know about Roy is that he is his equal in terms of brutality. And stashed inside the back of Roy's waistband is a hunting knife. One man will fall.

ARTHUR: I see my time here is up. I can respect a man's right to his own toilet. Just the other day I put a member of the Mexican mafia in the hospital for using the whites only toilet. Civil rights never reached prison. Never will. You wanna see races cling to their own? Lock em up inside four walls. Try and take away their dignity. See how fast they compete for the crown. Go with what you know. New world order, Roy. Any of this making sense?

(Arthur starts to go but stops in the doorway.)

But fuck if my curiosity ain't jumping off inside me. I'm a curious guy. It's a fault, I admit. But, I see here, there's two beds. One. Two. And I see there, that bathroom door is closed. And I'm looking at you, Roy, and I do apologize but I can't help intuit fear. And so I ask myself, why does this man fear me. Because you shouldn't. Unless you should. You say you don't fear me but I think you're lying. And I can't say I appreciate that. Especially since I've been up front with you since the moment we met. So I ask myself, why is this nice white man afraid of me....And so then I'm forced to look into his soul. And what I'm seeing I'm not liking. Not that it's any of my business but I'm thinking you're either a dick sucking queer or you got a nigger bitch hiding in that bathroom. Possibly a whore. Which even in my state of carnal desperation I would not deign to stick my dick in. And I ain't judging you, Roy.

But the more I look at you the more I'm coming up with queer. Tell me I'm wrong. Tell me you ain't a faggot. Cause in this instance I'd like to be wrong. Cause you seem like good people.

The Irish Curse
Martin Casella

Seriocomic
Rick, early 20s.

> *When a new guy to the Irish Curse Support Group is too afraid to go first for the evening's "share" session Rick, a smart, optimistic, fun-loving Staten Island stud who is studying sports medicine at a local NY college, offers to go first and show the new guy why they're there and what the meeting is all about. It's a support group for guys with abnormally small penises.*

RICK: *(standing, taking a moment)*

Hi. My name is Rick. Don't do the "Hi, Rick" thing.

(Pause.)

I'm twenty-two years old. I live on Staten Island. I go to Staten Island College. I'm studying sports medicine. And the reason I'm here is because -

(Pause.)

I got a small dick.

(Pause.)

I mean really small. Really. Small. Like small.

(Pause.)

Like from the children's menu.

(Pause.)

Growing up, I always heard it called the Irish Curse. It mostly only happens to us full-blooded Irish guys. Not all full-blooded Irish guys because my best bud Dylan is full-blooded Irish and he's hung like a giraffe.

(to Kieran)

We take showers together. After b-ball. Trust me.

(Pause.)

The Curse runs in my family. My father's got it. So do both my bros. One of them actually tried to off himself 'cause of it. Dumb fuck.

(to Kevin)

Sorry.

(back to Kieran)

He's okay now. The freak. He took pills.

(Pause.)

Everything I read about guys with small dicks goes on and on about how it's "all in their head" and "it doesn't make a difference" and my personal favorite, that "it ain't the meat it's the motion" bullshit –

(glancing at Kevin)

Sorry, Father.

(Pause.)

I just get really pissed off because those guys writing those columns are obviously walking around with a Happy Meal in their pants. And I would like to have dragged their collective asses down to the hospital where my bro was lying there with a tube down his throat and make them tell him to his face the size of his dick doesn't matter. It matters! It matters to me. It matters to him. It matters to all us guys who got royally fucked in that department. And Father, I'm not going to apologize for saying fucked.

(Pause.)

When I was growing up - I only ever saw my dad and my bros - so I never thought I was different from the other guys. Then when I got to middle school - that's when I found out I was a frigging freak -

Yeah. Right. Self esteem. "I am not my penis."

(grinning)

I only think I am.

(Pause.)

I have a lot of trouble not going there - to that dark place. I'm working on it. I even got my dad and both my bros working on it. But they're Irish. Optimism is not exactly a word in their dictionary.

(Pause.)

I love what I do. Studying the sports medicine. I'm a sports nut. B-ball. Hockey. I run.

(to Kieran)

Hanging around with athletes I learned this trick. I thought they were kidding but they all do it. Wear a jock. Always. Under your street clothes. Especially under jeans. It takes what you got. Shoves it up front and center. And I stuff it. A sock. Nice white sports tube. Loosely rolled. Great basket, huh?

(modeling for Kieran)

It's an illusion but most of Manhattan's walking around with more than what God gave 'em.

(Pause.)

Anyway. That's my sad story. Boo-hoo. "A million guys out there like me." "Least I got a penis." "It works, doesn't it?" "Yes it does." Any other comments and questions can be e-mailed to me at "Rick-I-Got-A-Small-Dick".com. Real website.

(making a fist, raising it)
Self-esteem!

The Irish Curse

Martin Casella

Seriocomic
Joseph, 40s

On the short side, stout and balding, this angry, liberal contracts lawyer from Savannah, Georgia (who now lives in New York) decides to tell the other members of the Irish Curse Support Group (for men with abnormally small penises) his theory about how everything, even American politics, all comes down to jealousy over the size of someone else's penis.

JOSEPH: And when you add in a little testosterone, no wonder we have guns and wars and bombs and terrorists - I mean, just look at the Middle East! You wanna sit those folks down and slap them all silly! How long have those Arabs and Jews been killing each other? And what for? Religion??! Land??!! Let's be honest, folks. It's not religion they've been fighting over. It's not land! What it boils down to is they're terrified that the Catholic next door or the Arab down the road's got a bigger weenie! I think, underneath, war's always been about that - don't you? I mean, medieval Europe against Islam, Commies against the West. I mean, why do you think people are still so upset about Vietnam? Really now, what does losing to a bunch of little Asian men in pajamas say about the size and power of the all-American wiener? There's always someone bigger and THAT's the fella you hate. You despise him. You want him to die in a fiery car crash going ninety miles an hour on the expressway. You want to drop missiles on his mosque! Blow up his buildings! Kill his women! Not because you hate him - oh no! Because you hate the size of his dick. Because it's longer and thicker and harder and hairier. What do you think the South is all about! What do you think those pick-up trucks are about? And Confederate flags and swords and guns. They can't even admit they lost a war that was over over a hundred and fifty years ago because it would mean some Goddamned Yankee had a bigger wiener! Really, that's what war is all about! Mine's bigger! Mine's fatter. Mine shoots farther. Wish they'd start putting that in the history books!!! I can see George W. Bush sitting in the Oval office going through secret Iraqi files and photographs, having a triple shit fit because ol' Saddam's pecker is twice the size of his!! That's why all those asshole Republicans hated President Clinton so much. Because unlike Mr. Bush, what an appropriate name, he didn't have to start a war to show everyone just how huge his penis is. All those guys – Mitch McConnell and John Boehner – know how you actually pronounce his name? "Boner!" You know the guy I mean! The one with the spray-on orange tan - he looks like a fucking Oompa-Loompa. All those arrogant middle-aged white men with bad hair and chicken dicks - they can't stand it! Because if ol' Barack is using his Democratic weenie for the reason it was actually invented, that must mean it's bigger than all the rest of those Republican weenies combined! And let's not forget the fact he's black. You know what they say about black men, Stephen. He must have a dick the size of Connecticut! That's why they're trying to destroy him. Starting those rumors he's an Arab. That he wasn't born here! That he's a socialist. That he's Hitler. Because they're all so Goddamn jealous of Obama and his big dick! Because American men can't stand it when the other guy has what they don't!

The Irish Curse
Martin Casella

Dramatic
Kevin, early 50s.

> *Father Kevin Shaughnessy, a Catholic priest originally from Boston and the moderator of the Irish Curse Support Group (for men with abnormally small penises), has been egged on by the group members to tell them about his own shortcomings, and how they changed the outcome of the one romantic interlude he had before he became a priest.*

KEVIN: There was one girl. She was Portuguese. Her family owned a bakery. She was beautiful. And Catholic. She was in love with me.
> *(takes a moment, acting it all out, loving the spotlight.)*

So there I was - at seventeen - after having suffered through all the teasing and laughing in the locker room - and there was this girl - and we liked each other - I thought, well, maybe it's okay after all - maybe girls don't care about stuff like that. That's what the magazines say. They interview women about what they like. The size of your willie's usually about number ten down the list. All I know is Lucy kept pressuring me to "do it." "I wanna do it," she'd say. "Let's do it." "All my friends are doing it." So we hid out in the storage room at the bakery. After it closed. We started fooling around on the floor and pretty soon we were covered all in white flour. I was kissing her and we were both going a little nuts and we got undressed and she had this gorgeous thin body and I was standing there with my stiffy. Well, she took one look at the "plump stump" and started shrieking. "Where's the rest of it?!! That can't be all!!! There's gotta be more!!!!" She didn't know any better. She came from a big family - she'd seen her brothers naked, I guess - apparently, they were all regular guys. I wish she had laughed. I could have handled that. Because of the guys at school. She just shrieked. Like she was disgusted. Like it made her sick.

The Irish Curse
Martin Casella

Dramatic
Keiran, late 20s-early 30s.

This sweet, sincere and terribly conflicted young Irish immigrant finally tells the other men in the Irish Curse Support Group (for men with abnormally small penises) why he needs their help, and how his upcoming marriage has nearly driven him mad with anxiety and fear about the size of his shillelagh.

KIERAN: After Kelly and I went out a few times, we talked about having sex. She's a nice Catholic girl but like most Catholic girls - I had to put her off!

(pause)

Said I wanted to be a gentleman. She thought I was gay. I assured her I wasn't. Said I respected her and that I would like to wait until we were married. She wasn't keen on that but she agreed. Every now and then, she'd hint around she wouldn't mind if we did. She was honest. Told me she wasn't a virgin. I told her I was. That seemed to excite her.

I couldn't tell her why I was a virgin I couldn't. Especially since she'd had experience. We did other things. Sexual things. Just never with my willie. When we finally decided to get married, I was in a frenzy. Being married meant sex. Real sex. I had to get some help. I went to bookstores, magazines racks, anything I could get my hands on. I'd sit at the computer for hours. Any website that had the word penis in it, I was there. I went to this one place - well, it's supposed to be for guys in our situation - to make you feel better - feel normal - I mean, the home page has these pictures of guys with little willies - little? - Holy Mother of God, they're non-existent! I mean, I thought this page was supposed to make me feel better! I felt worse! Like I'm looking at this page of FREAKS! The worst part was, at the bottom of the page, there were these photos of fellas with huge willies - gigantic willies - titanic, leviathan willies - I didn't know willies came that big! There was this one fella - he had a fourteen inch willie - fourteen inches - soft - Jesus - ! I ask you! Is that the sum total of what this poor lad's gonna be known for his entire life? Well, as I said, since the engagement I've been looking for help. For almost a year. The wedding is Saturday. My willie's as tiny as it ever was.

(pause)

That's about all I have to say.

The Language Archive
Julia Cho

Dramatic
George, mid-late 30s

> *George is a philologist who studies and tries to document languages which are almost extinct. His wife has just left him and here, in direct address to the audience, he talks about how that made him feel.*

GEORGE: It's a very curious thing when your wife leaves you. The world slows down.
Words become...*(lugubriously:)* lugubrious.
My heart was beating very loudly.
But instead of thumping, every beat was saying,
"Take it back, take it back, take it back."
Just like that. Like a rhythm.
And it was so loud that I couldn't hear anything else,
even my own thoughts, whatever they might have been.
And I was sure she must be hearing it too.
It was as thunderous as horse hooves, louder than tanks,
how could anyone not hear it?
Take it back, take it back, take it back.
Or if she couldn't hear it, I thought surely she must be able to see it, the words running like ticker tape through the whites of my eyes, like those old cartoons when the cat is hit on the head with a mallet. Take it back, take it back.
My whole body was begging her. Take it back, take it back—
If you go, it'll destroy me. Take it back, take it back— I'll be a city in ruins—
Take it back, take it back— It's not too late—
Take it back, take it back—
My whole body was shouting it. Couldn't SHE HEAR IT?
Why wasn't she saying something???

The Language Archive
Julia Cho

George, mid-late 30s

George is a philogist who studies and tries to document languages which are almost extinct. His wife Mary has just announced that he is leaving him.

GEORGE: Mary. Do you know how languages die? One. Natural disaster. A typhoon, say, knocking out an entire village that is the only place where a certain language is spoken. Two. Social assimilation. When speakers of two languages choose the more socially dominant one to the point where their children speak only that language and lose the other one completely. I speak many languages. But I do not speak the one my grandmother spoke. Why? Because my parents didn't really speak it. And didn't care if I really spoke it. Because it was not the socially dominant language. Thus: I never cared to learn it. It was the one language I never cared to learn. And now it's too late. So, Mary.

There is a certain language...our language...and. If you don't come back, I can't speak it anymore. Do you understand? We are the only two speakers of that language. And if you don't come back, the language will die. And no one on earth will ever speak it again. For instance, the phrase: "Will somebody please take out the garbage?" Depending on tone it can mean: "You jerk, take out the garbage!" Or, "I feel lonely." Or, "It's our anniversary next week, I hope you remember." Or, "A world without you is unimaginable to me."

Mary. Mary. Will somebody please take out the garbage?

The Language of Trees
Steven Levenson

Dramatic
Denton, early 30s

Denton, an idealistic American translator, is sent to a Middle East combat zone as a private contractor. He leaves behind his emotionally fragile wife, Loretta, and their seven-year old son, Eben. After a nightmarish morning raid that went terribly awry, he writes a letter to his wife.

DENTON: We raided a village east of the capital this morning. So early the air was still black, so thick you couldn't see the fingers in front of your face. We all sat very quiet in the Humvee. Not a sound anywhere, besides for our breathing. The in and out of six men breathing in the dark.

We hit the ground. Hard. We break down doors. We shatter windows with rifles and fists. We burst into people's homes and snap them awake with guns pressed into tired faces.

And I am caught in a volley of words. I catch them in my left ear. They slide in, something wet and hard, like a finger coated in saliva. The words, they spin and they tumble on the soft lining of my brain. A matter of seconds. And they leap forward from my mouth, remade, re-crafted into something sensible, something bright and clear. An icicle of meaning.

Things are moving fast now, so fast, no chance to stop. No chance to breathe. We do not breathe. Broken windows. Cracked doorframes. Guns in sleepy faces. Icicles of meaning. Fingers in my ear. Guns in sleepy faces. Broken windows. The smell of mud everywhere. You gag from it. The adrenaline is thundering, pounding and booming faster and louder and louder and louder and louder.

And then suddenly it all goes quiet.

For a moment. Nothing.

And then ... everything explodes.

People are screaming. Children and women and old men are screaming through my ears. Into my mouth. We are running. We are breathing so hard. And running. The soldiers are running and they are shooting. The bullets are deafening. They are dancing in the air, all around us, a swarm of bullets, like flies, these huge flies dancing, burrowing themselves into people's arms and legs and necks and chests and faces. These gigantic fucking flies. *(Long (Pause.)* I have a helmet now. And a gun. Temporarily. Just until things calm down. It should only be a matter of days, they say. Besides, it's only a precaution. Don't worry. Please. *(Beat.)* Don't show this letter to Eben. *(Short Pause.)* *(The lights, already dim, fade slowly.)* It's strange. I woke up last night and for a second I thought I was home. In our bed. I turned to kiss your shoulder.. My mouth still tastes like metal.

Lascivious Something
Sheila Callaghan

Dramatic
Boy, 14

A 14 year old boy steps into the spotlight. He addresses us as his mother and father look on.

BOY: July 28, 1978.

Your mouth is chomping wint-o-green after wint-o-green right now. You're in the kitchen surrounded by bills. I can hear you through the vents as I write this. You chew faster when you're anxious. Maybe you're chewing as you read this. Illegible. Crossed-out. I know this is sloppy but I wanted to preserve each thought as it left my pen to give an accurate record of illegible. Crossed-out crossed-out scribble wanted to.

But first, business. You should sell anything that has some value, like my bike and myrecords and my books. Not my hi-fi. The left speaker is broken. I left my pot in the top drawer for you, but it's kind of old. Scribble scribble crossed-out forget it, that wasn't funny. My clothes are probably worthless, they were when we bought them.

Now here's the crossed-out part. I know we said I'd try but illegible crossed-out illegible not changing, nothing changes and it won't. Like remember how I had that so-called break-through and I told Dr. Randy that the world felt fake, and that I was the only one who knew it was fake? I still feel this way, but it's much worse now because crossed-out scribble sorry, my knuckle hurts.

But knowing this is not true and feeling it in my heart are two different things. And I can't stop, I play every single scenario over and over in my head only it's worse now because I do it over really small things. "If I brush my teeth this morning, THIS will happen. If I don't, THIS will happen." Or like, "If I blink my left eye, THIS will happen. If I blink my right, THIS will." And then I think, if all the different outcomes for every single tiny thing are endless, how can ANYTHING be real? And then the ringing starts just like before and then I get weightless and I'm shaking and throwing up again. And the crossed-out panic doesn't ever illegible. Especially at night. My heart beats so hard my eyeballs bounce. It would be cool if it didn't make me illegible.

You just yawned really loud. It was funny. In a few seconds your head will be on the table, and you'll be drooling onto the phone bill. I'll touch your head on my way out, so maybe you'll still feel my hand there when you wake up.

Oh, do you remember Colleen, the girl from the Y who used to write with her toes to impress people? You were right, I did have sex with her. But only once. She smelled like paper. I always felt bad about that lie.

Don't save this letter, okay mom? Just read it once. Then burn it.

Love you,

August

Local Nobody
Nicole Pandolfo

Seriocomic
Lou, 50

Lou is a former Hells Angel who owns the local bar. Married, but likes getting laid whenever by whomever. Here, he is speaking with regular patron Sal at the bar that he runs. Sal has told Lou that his father died that morning. Lou is looking after Sal to make sure he doesn't drink himself to death. Sal asks how Lou's daughter, Emily, is doing.

LOU: Emily? She's alright man. She got all A's on her report card. She's a pain in the ass. The other day, I got a phone call from the principal. She and this slut in training, Mackenzie- Wait, before I go on, can I just say, what is it with the gay-ass names people are naming their kids lately. What the fuck? Mackenzie, and there's this kid in her class named Sparkle. I swear to fucking God man, some dipshit in this town named their kid Sparkle. Anyway, Emily and this Mackenzie mini-slut pull this little boy, Eddie, into the girls bathroom and they do a little show and tell. They get Eddie to pull his fucking dick out, get a good look at it, watch him pee, and then they drop their pants and show him their fucking junk. Some teacher walked in on them and they made Emily spend the rest of the day sitting in the principal's office discussing "inappropriate conduct." Like, what the fuck does that mean to a eight year old? I told Bernice, "this is your fucking fault for breast feeding that kid until she was six."Apparently it helps with brain development or some shit like that. I don't really know how sucking on tits that long makes your brain better, but Bernice swears by it. But look, now she's a fucking pervert. Anyway, now I gotta go beat the shit out of Eddie's dad, just to prove a point. I don't want Emily growing up to be a whore.

The Long Red Road
Brett C. Leonard

Dramatic
Sammy, 32

Sammy is in South Dakota, talking to a Native American bartender. He was involved in a tragic car accident years ago in his home state of Kansas and has been on the run ever since.

SAMMY: I wake up a booth sittin' a group a' U.S. Marines I ain't never met in a bar I ain't never been - "Excuse me", I slur, I say, "excuse me, SIR! - death before dishonor, SIR! - but where the fuck'm I at? Yeah I know it's a BAR, Jarhead, but where the fuck is the bar LOCATED?! Tijuana?! Wellmotherfuck an' goddamn, I'm so long a friggin' blackout I come to we at war with fuckin' Mexico. All I know's Flat-top, we better the fuck win this one - y'all ain't win this one, I'm off ta Ireland, fish fer my supper... fer my SUFFER - piss my pants in goddamn peace, no judgements, no looky-loos, no johnny-laws neither...Judge not lest ye..." Lemme get two more, Clifton... Lila Itomni. This lil' fuck Flat-top with his bigger flat-top leatherneck fucks aside him, he go "You been out quite awhile, pally, welcome back, but now you, uh...now maybe's time ya head back home." Believe this prick? I bust'm open his fuckin' earhole a bottle a' tequila, tellin' me what I should or should not do. I hate mothafuckers tell me what I should or shouldn't do. His buddies start wailin', whoopin' the shit outta me - "U.S. Marine Corps! U.S.M.C.!" - they got blood pourin' out my goddamn forehead inta my mouth, I'm curled up, a lil' ball, tryin' juss...tryin' keep my brains spillin' out - I hear a rib crack, then another...then a, uh... whaja call, right here? (re: his shoulder)- hear that shit snap in half too - all I see's black boots an' green camouflage, stompin', kickin' - legs, boots, blood - "kick his ass, YA DRUNK SUMBITCH! - teach'm a goddamn LESSON - U.S.M.C., U.S.A., U.S.A.". I'm there tryin' ta enjoy a goddamn drink! Thirty two years...trailer park-flophouse-carseat¬-alleyways...never had no run-in no goddamned Armed Force. Cross the frickin' border first time come one/ come all try an' get me. There's too many goddamn Americans in Mexico - but ya never see that shit in the news, do ya!? Ya never goddamn hear about that! But not here, right? Not here with the Indians. Ain't no need for no Canada, no Mexico, no nothin'...no borders...no po-lice. Ain't no

America never gonna find us right here. Ain't that right, Cliff? Ain't it right?

The Long Red Road
Brett C. Leonard

Dramatic
Bob, 36

> *Bob is from Kansas. He is talking to his brother Sam's girlfriend, Annie.*
> *The brothers haven't seen each other in nine years; not since Sam, while*
> *driving drunk, got into a car accident which resulted in the death of one of*
> *his daughters and the maiming of his wife. His other daughter survived. She*
> *is present as Bob talks about her father to Annie.*

BOB: You even know a goddamn thing about my brother, huh? Or maybe ya just know the things he told you an' left the rest ta figger out in the dark? I could shed the light, if ya like. Cuz he's opposite a' you, boy - look atchya... deviled eggs, "could I get you this?, you want more a' that?" My brother, well... he ain't like that. You save, he abandons. He run off his whole goddamn life, from he was a lil shit back ta the crib - back his sixth birthday - six years old momma an' daddy get that spoiled sumbitch a brand new Evel Knievel red¬white-an'-blue bicycle, with ribbons an' a horn, an'... I never got no bicycle, never. An' he get a big ol' party ta go with - twenny, twenny-five kids, parents, couple teachers come too. Lil' spoiled Sam-Sam, I'm the older brother, I ain't never got shit. Not shit, but some late night visits and a bed in the barn while lil' spoiled Sam-Sam got his own goddamn room in the house with his own lock on the goddamn door. I'm sleepin' the barn one eye open, Sammy's Evel¬fuckin'-Knievel with a ticket ta the rodeo. An' that spoiled¬-get-his-way-six-year-old-sonuvabitch - everybody singin' an' clappin' "happy birthday ta you, happy birthday ta Sam"... Sammy hop aboard his red-white-blue Evel Knievel, honk the horn an' ride off. "Bye, Sam, bye, Wow, lookit'm go - yippee!" An' then we all just sit 'round an' wait. An' wait some more. "When we gonna cut the cake?" "Shut up Bobby, we waitin' on Sam." "When we gonna pin the tail on the donkey?" "Shut up, Bobby, wait for Sam." "But when we gonna...Shut up Bobby, wait for Sam." But he's SAM, see? He don't care others care 'bout him cuz he ain't care 'bout others. An' the party gets dark, people get tired a' waitin'. They start sayin' their goodbyes. No more party an' still no Sam. Nobody left but mom, dad, and ME ta clean everything up. *(Beat.)* Sammy come home three days later. Three days an' three nights. Said he was in a cornfield. Said he was thinkin'. Said he din't know no one was expectin' him to return to the party and he hopes we all had a good time. He was off thinkin'... about life, he said. Six years old. Thinkin' about his own life, ta be sure. (re: Tasha) This one here the same goddamn way. No concern 'bout no one but theyselves.

The Long Red Road

Brett C. Leonard

Dramatic
Sammy, 32

> *Sammy is in South Dakota, talking to a Native American bartender. He was involved in a tragic car accident years ago in his home state of Kansas and has been on the run ever since.*

SAMMY: YOU AIN'T KNOW SHIT, YOU AIN'T KNOW A GODDAMN THING! SHE WAS FOUR YEARS OLD! FOUR GODDAMN YEARS! Which makes her what?, what's that make her, Cliff, the dead one? I s'pose that makes her she ain't NO goddamn age is she? She stopped ageing. Comin' home drunk from a friend a theirs birthday -- their Momma was there, lotta other parents there too. Not me though, I didn't make it, no. I was at a bar. Time pass I go pick 'em up, get there safe an' fine, alls I gotta do now's get 'em home same way. Same twenny-five miles I drove drunk an' blacked-out more'n two hundred, two thousand times. I wa'n't bout ta give my wife the keys, though, no, I knew best, of course, always did. Told'r "I'm fine, leave me alone", told'r "Don't try to control me - tellin' me what I should or should not do, I don't like that, blah-blah." An' all I remember's after that's headlights comin' face-on... an' me turnin' the wheel like this, this way, to my left... bein' sure ta protect myself from the impact. Bein' sure ta protect my side a' the car. An' then I run. I din't stick around for my family, I din't stick 'round try an' help nobody in no other car neither. I didn't stick around. Hopped me a freight, never turned back. An' you wanna know the best part? Huh? The best part? When I was lookin' at my wife...with the whole goddamn car crashed into her legs... my twin girls behind me, one dead, the other pleadin' with her big scared eyes... The best part, I thought, well...here's your proof, Sam...here's what you was waitin' on... your CONFIRMATION... You are a terrible human being. Run, Sam - run. Now's your chance, before they learn the truth about you. Hell, now's THEIR chance - Go on. Let 'em be, Sammy. Go ruin someone else's life. *(Beat.)* Screw it, gimme a drink.

Love Town
Michael Kaplan

Seriocomic
Lyle, 36

> *Lyle is a surfer-stoner-jack-of-all-trades pushing against the responsibilities of*
> *marriage and middle age. He and his wife run a little business that creates*
> *magical moments for tourists. In this speech, Lyle explains to his friend Karl*
> *how he got distracted from the latest job.*

LYLE: I had this big deal to set up. Midnight moonlight proposAL: Mindy's all torqued because I keep getting the names wrong: Frank & Coretta. Frank & Coretta. Get the flowers and the champagne and the chocolates in a big ass basket out on Otter Point for FRANK & CORETTA. So I get out there, I set it up perfect, I go down to the beach and the beach is mobbed. The grunion were running last night. You ever do the grunion run? They're little stupid fish. You can't use nets. You can't use poles. You gotta catch them with your bare hands, they're coming in on the low tide to mate. Lay their eggs, fertilize their eggs, get the hell out. So they're screwing and spawning and we're grabbing and splashing, everybody gets all sexed up. And the fog rolls in and nobody can see, and it just turns into this wet bump and grind and next thing I know I'm kissing somebody. I'm making out with this sweet-smelling silhouette. You know what happened? My dick woke up. My dick has been numb for eight months, I get into bed with Mindy my eyes are shut I'm spinning the wheel of women. Someone from the past, some chunky butt sitting on my lap in college—anything to get it going. And suddenly I'm on the freezing flipping beach at midnight and my dick is beating on the gates. I'm alive! I'M ALIVE IN HERE! It was other women, Karl. That's an asshole thing to say—that's like not the conclusion we're EVER supposed to have. But Jesus Christ, Karl. Other women. That's what I've been missing.

Matthew and the Pastor's Wife
Robert Askins

Dramatic
Matthew, mid to late forties

Matthew is speaking to Dorothy, his accountability partner as well as his pastor's wife. He is confessing the particulars of a disastrous seduction, all the while trying to seduce her, which proves to a dangerous thing to do.

MATTHEW: Seems that's how wantin starts with me. Eyes are okay. Lookin is nice but it's the thought of a thing between my teeth that drives me out too far. There was this Mexican girl used to clean the house. We talk about this. Feel like I tole you bout this. I lost the job over at B&B. I was spendin too much time round the house. She come over and we'd talk Mexican a little. You know, Que onda way? Todo bien. She couldn'ta been moren 19. Maybe younger. She'd come over in the mornin. bout ten. I'd have a beer turn on reruns an some shit. Frasier. Friends. Matlock. She clean and I'd just watch her. Wasn't too long she started wearin lacy underwear. Now I'm not an under wear kinda guy. But... The way it cut into her body a she bent from the waist. The thought of it in my teeth. Made my mouth water. I got to drinkin in the a.m. Got to to turnin off the T.V. got to givin her beer. She was grateful. We got to leavin. She'd finish and I'd go job huntin. We'd meet in bars in the afternoon. I'd spend all day lost in her, wonderin at her construction. Spreadin her fingers wide to study the fine skin stretch between them. Takin measure of her waist with my hand. It always is a wonder to me. Women's bellies. Seems like there ain't enough square footage just to pack the guts in. We was talkin. I's learnin bout the way she thinks. See that's the real mutherfucker of it. Women think different. Soft in someway like velvet. It can get to the point where the talkin gets thick. Like running your tongue through thick thick soft black. Fillin your mouth too much. Softness and warmth spillin over your chin. Drip to the chest. I know why you don wanna meet in you office.

Motherhouse
Victor Lodato

Dramatic
Ross, 30s

> *An agitated Ross discusses his frustrations about his mother's house—and her furniture arrangement—with his friend Clive (another man in his thirties, who also lives with his mother). Ross's swagger and manic energy are partially his nature, but amplified perhaps by drugs.*

ROSS: I didn't recognize anything. You know? I didn't be at my mother's house for like a year. And she done it all over. Same stuff, but she done it all around, the placement— you know what I'm saying? Messed it up. I was confused. I was truly confused. You want a chair to be where you remember there a chair. And you don't want a chair where there should be nothing. Then you can't hardly walk through the house. All these chairs in my way. Cause there a certain way I used to move through that house. And now she done messed that up. Chair in the hallway. I mean, why she got a chair in the hallway now? Who gonna sit on that? What, she can't walk from one end a the hall to the other without having to sit her ass down? I mean she old, but she ain't that old. And I keep tripping on that chair—you know, get up in the dark, go the bathroom—I, I can't keep it in my mind that it's there. And it go against the way I move. Go against my body. And then the couch, she got it broken now in two parts, like a V *(illustrates with his hands)*, like that, because that couch a sectional, it goes this way or that way, however you wanna do it. And she used to have it in one good long straight line, all the parts, all one way, the way a couch should be. Now she got it in this V. I can't even sit on that. Feel like it's closing in on you. I sit in that house, on that couch, and I get so—I don't know. *(Pause)* Why can't it just be the way it used to be? Why can't she just leave it that way? Cause the thing is: you remember something, you want to stay with that, you don't want to improve upon that. You got the idea of the house down, the idea of the house. That is in you mind from way back, and she gotta go and fuck with that. Doing it around like it someplace else. Like she got no respect for how the house lives in my mind

Office Hours

A. R. Gurney

Seriocomic
Hal, 30s

Hal teaches a section of a college class on the Great Books which is a core requirement but which may be in danger of being eliminated from the curriculum. Here, he is talking to some other teachers about how he livens up his lectures in an effort to get his students to care about Homer.

HAL: Want to hear what I did yesterday? They always sit up when the subject is sex. So I reminded them that the hero, Odysseus, is involved in this long love affair with the beautiful sea-nymph Calypso on his way home from Troy. But finally he's had enough. The affair is over. Homer says, "He yearned to see the smoke from his hearth-fire rising."

The question is, why does Homer say that? Why doesn't he say that Odysseus yearns to cradle his beautiful wife in his arms after twenty years? Or why doesn't he yearn to see his only son whom he left as a baby? Why does he yearn – what a wonderful word, "yearn" – why does Homer focus on the "smoke from his hearth-fire rising" ? Ask your students, and see what they say. I offered them a proposition. I said Odysseus' desire to go home is as natural as smoke rising from a fire. Smoke rises, men go home. The burning hearth is the natural center of active domestic life, the rising smoke a universal physical phenomenon. A man's yearning to go home is equally natural, equally universAL: How about that? If you ask it right, they might come up with something better. Tim … Don't you yearn to see the smoke from your own hearth fire rising? Or at least to hear the hum of your microwave? And though your wife may be a motor mouth, and your baby an alarm clock, don't you miss them when you spend the night here? And don't you think your students have their own yearnings, now they're here, beginning their own adventures in a foreign land? So get them talking about home, man! Ask what home means to them. And then bring them back to Odysseus. Because after he's embraced his son, screwed his wife, and killed the guys who made their moves on her, Homer tells us he has to leave again. Ask them why. They won't know. Tell them to stick with the course because it will all make sense next spring when we get to Dante. Suspense, man. Throw in some suspense.

Office Hours

A. R. Gurney

Seriocomic
Jason, 30s

*Jason teaches a section of a college class on the Great Books which is a core
requirement but which may be in danger of being eliminated from the
curriculum. One of the Great Books they study is the Bible. Here, he is telling
his students about a realization he had when reading the letters of Paul.*

JASON: Well, gang, we've been off to a tricky start in our second semester.
In our first class, as we picked up the Book of Genesis, I declared I was
a devout atheist, and spent the next two days defending the idea of
evolution against what I call the Evangelistas.
(He eyes them in the audience)
When we turned to Exodus, one of our Orthodox Jewish students
announced that I was clueless about the meaning of the Covenant and
the Law, and several of his co-religionists complained that I had ignored
the implications of the Holocaust and the state of Israel.
(He indicates where the Jewish contingent is)
When we finally found ourselves in the Gospel According to Mark,
members of the Campus Crusade for Christ …
(Sees them)
… insisted that it was simply the sacred account of the Son of God
entering the world, and we should approach it only on our knees. And
just today, when we're supposed to be talking about the Epistles of Paul
…
(takes out a document)
…I received a notice from the Course Committee giving us
permission to skip Paul entirely, on the grounds that he is …
(reading)
… anti-semitic."
(slight pause)
O. K. But since I've already assigned the man, let's talk about him
briefly before we leap across the centuries to Saint Augustine. I admit
that Paul, like most converts, can be a royal pain in the ass. And some
of his phrases, like circumcision of the heart, are ludicrous to men and
irrelevant to women. Still, let's look at the last few lines from his Epistle

to the Romans.

(opens his Bible to a tagged page. Reads)

"All the commandments are summed up in this sentence: you shall love your neighbor as yourself. Love does no wrong to a neighbor; therefore love is the fulfilling of the law."

(to audience)

See? There's your Jewish Law – that complicated list of do's and don'ts - converted simply into Love. It's a radical new thought, and I have to say an admirable one. .

(returns to text)

Paul continues: "Besides this, you know how it is high time for you to wake from sleep."

(looks up)

Possibly Paul is admitting that he puts people to sleep. And perhaps I should admit the same thing.

(singles out a member of the audience)

But isn't he also saying that life itself will seem like a sleep until Christ wakes us up?

(returns to the text)

"For the sun is on the horizon, the night is far gone, the day is at hand. Let us then cast off the works of darkness and put on the armor of light."

(looks up)

How can we not go for that, gang? It's pure poetry. Paul asks us to toss off the moth-eaten blankets of ignorance, and get dressed in the glittering armor of our new belief. Sleep, wake, night, day, dark, light – I dunno. You can't say it better than that..

(returns to text)

And then Paul sends his blessings to all the people in Rome who have been working their butts off, risking the Coliseum just to spread the word. And he gets personAL: He names names..

(reads)

Phoebe ,,, And Rufus …And Julia … And Hey! look at this, folks..

(displays his Bible)

Here's Jason. Jason happens to be my name. He names me! And he blesses each of us and prays for our happiness.

(looks up)

Look at me. I'm tearing up – as I always do when I read that.

(blows his nose, dries his eyes)

So: I'm beginning to think that this letter from Paul to his friends in Rome, written by a man who will soon be crucified there, contains probably the first moment of warmth in Western Literature since Plato's description of the death of Socrates three hundred years before. Read it yourself and see if it doesn't shake you up.

Pigmalion
Mark Dunn

Comic
Cal Pickering, late 40s

Cal Pickering is professorial friend and colleague to "Kudzu League" professor Henry Higgins (and plays a role similar, in this respect, to the Colonel Pickering of Shaw's classic). He shares many of Higgins' views in terms of how he regards those less academically inclined or intellectually curious (although, he is somewhat the softer version of Higgins). In this monologue, Cal is trying to explain to Eliza Doolittle and her friend Tiffany Box why Henry would be unwilling to teach Eliza how to speak with less of a redneck delivery. He takes this opportunity to examine why southern speakers of English abuse the language so. Though he thinks he's doing his friend Henry a favor by this explication, the perception from Eliza and Tiffany is that Henry, though perhaps justified in his views, is elitist, academically snobbish, and really quite a jerk.

CAL: How should I put this? Every stroll that Henry and I take through every Mississippi Delta town we visit – and we've visited just about every one of them -- ends up with this one here pursing his lips and tutting like an old school marm and expounding ad infinitum on that same tired old subject: how a certain class of southerner has lost every last vestige of his affiliation with his native tongue.

Te rural southerner can't speak the language, or at least can't speak it in such a way as to be clearly understood and respected. The English language: it's the most sophisticated, the most complex, the most deliciously-nuanced language in the world – says he – but it's been largely abandoned by a sizeable segment of the American South. I you've said it once, you've said it a thousand times, Henry: give me one of these redneck, hillbilly, dirty-faced Dixieland ground-feeders and after six weeks, I could pass him off as the governor of Mississippi. But it isn't going to happen. Because most southerners are lazy. Why else do they drawl? Why else do their tongues just loll about in their mouths as if forced enunciation would put them into a coma for all the exertion?

The Rant
Andrew Case

Dramatic
Alexander Stern, early 40s

> *Stern is a crime reporter for a New York tabloid covering the shooting of an unarmed black teenager by an NYPD officer. He got the investigator on the case to leak details of the shooting and printed them, and in response the police department leaked embarrassing details about the victim and his mother. Pausing to consider whether what he has done is appropriate, he addresses the audience.*

ALEXANDER: Tell me what you believe about these two cases and I will prove you are a bigot. If you believe that despite Ms. Farber's bruises Kobe was framed, and DNA be damned the lacrosse players are guilty, you have decided, with the AmNews, that black voices are to be trusted more than white. If you believe Kobe is the rapist, if the semen from three different men in Ms. Farber's underwear gives you no pause, and you think the Duke lacrosse players hired two strippers for their drunken brawl and behaved like perfect gentlemen, you are a racist, believing the white accuser and the white accused.

If you think both women are lying, you are a sexist, and if you take both women at their word, you are biased against men. That's it — there is no answer to get you off the hook. You believe the women, you believe the men, you believe the whites, or you believe the blacks.

And yet, one of those four scenarios is the truth. If we could ever find out the truth, it would vindicate one set of bigots or the other. Believing that facts and evidence can be trusted leaves you unready for the inevitable moment when the facts align with prejudice. White cops bully black kids. Black kids join gangs and com-mit crimes. Firemen steal jewelry from the wreckage of homes. The conventional wisdom of the Upper West Side cocktail soiree is offensive to the block party in Tottenville. And vice versa.

So I no longer believe in facts. I believe in leverage. I quoted from a confidential statement from Ms. Reeves, and the next morning I had a confidential 911 recording from the police department, Ms. Reeve's voice dire, desperate. I had a sealed criminal record, a whole collection of secrets - and people keep secrets from each other because they are true.

And people on both sides dig in, and accuse each other of racism for doubting a black woman or racism for believing her, and at the end of a long string of bylines I will close the case, like so many before it, with a final footnote that we will never know the truth.

And Denise Reeves and Charles Simmons and Sergeant Clarke will go on remembering what may have happened on a porch on Pitkin Avenue and take solace only in the fact that if I say the name Katelyn Farber or Crystal Gail. Mangum in two years, you will struggle to remember who I mean.

Rantoul and Die
Mark Roberts

Dramatic
Gary, 40s. Thick Midwestern accent.

Rallis is distraught that his wife, Debbie, wants to end the marriage. He attempts suicide and is left in a vegetative state. Wracked with guilt, Debbie tells her lover, the menacingly charismatic Gary, that she will no longer leave her husband. Gary responds by choking Debbie nearly to death. This monologue occurs immediately after he releases her from his grip.

GARY: I don't need you. You hear what I'm saying? I am done with you. Right now. As of this minute. As I was laying on top of you, choking the life out of you, I realized then and there. You're not for me. You're not a healthy person. I don't know why I didn't see it from the very start. You're nothing but trouble, and that's all you ever have been. I am officially over you. Seriously. It's like the clouds have parted, and I'm feeling like myself again. I found me. Gary's back. He's been lost for a little while, but he's back. And I ain't gonna let you drag me through the mud no more. Them days are done. And to tell you the truth, I'm not even mad at you anymore. You know what I feel for you? Sadness. I feel sorry for you. Because, you are a lost individual and I'm not judging you. I just pity you. And I hope that you get it together someday. I do. But, that's gonna have to be on somebody else's watch, cause I wash my hands of you. Man. I have clarity for the first time in a long time. It's like, I can see better, or something. Colors look brighter, and the world seems more filled with possibilities. I'm glad I got out of this when I did, because a woman like you just drags a man down. That's who you are. No offense, but you're a piece of trash. I feel sorry for you. I really do. You have no idea who you are. You're a sad, manipulative creature. Unexamined life, bitch! Good luck with that! Getting rid of you is the smartest thing I've ever done.

A Russian Play

Don Nigro

Seriocomic
Nikolay, 31,

Nikolay is a successful Russian novelist and playwright, who has come to spend part of his summer at the Volkonsky estate in the Russian provinces. Here, in the gazebo on a summer day, he finds himself alone with Anya, the youngest Volkonsky daughter, an innocent girl who loves art and the theatre and desperately wants to become a writer. She admires him and his work with a deep passion that embarrasses him. He is not really a bad fellow at heart, but he's cynical, bored, knows that his work is superficial and worthless, and his self-absorption leads him to be oblivious of the fact that he is crushing this poor girl's hopes rather brutally. He really doesn't mean to. He just doesn't see it until it's too late.

NIKOLAY: I'll tell you what the theatre is about. It's about people like you who are always wanting things, and trying to get things, and failing to get them, and suffering. And that's just the actors, but it's also true about the characters they play. Or they get what they want, and then suffer because they find they didn't want what they thought they wanted after all. Or they get what they want and then lose it and suffer some more. In a tragedy, we identify with the people who are suffering, although a good deal of the pleasure we get is because we're happy they're not us. In a comedy, on the other hand, we stand back and snarl at them and cough, and this mixture of snarling and coughing we call laughter, and tell ourselves it's a good thing, but it's not. Suffering is not a good thing---Dostoyevsky was an idiot---and laughter is not a good thing either, because laughter is cruel, and cruelty is not a good thing, because ultimately it's boring, like everything else. In the end it's all futility. Absolute folly and futility. If you want to write, fine, then write. It doesn't make a bit of difference one way or the other to me or anyone else on earth. Nobody really cares about anybody else's writing. Nobody can stop you from writing if you really can't help it. But if you imagine that it will make you happy, you're a fool. And if you think it will make anybody else happy, you're insane. What kind of jackass is made happy by Shakespeare? People dressing up in other people's clothing and then not recognizing each other? How stupid can these people be? Are they all cross-eyed? If anybody ever put on a pair of spectacles, half of those plays would be over in the first act. People strangling each other and cutting off their hands. Really. The theatre is like a charnel house. It may seduce a person into caring about it for a while, but in the end, it's all rubbish, like everything else. All writing is rubbish. Even life and joy and hope aren't really life and joy and hope. They're actually death and suffering and despair as seen by an idiot. There, I've just come dangerously close to quoting Shakespeare---clear evidence that I haven't an original thought in my head. I'm usually more clever than this, but I haven't slept in weeks, and when I do finally nod off for a moment, I have horrendous nightmares about soup made of ox eyes, and the soup is looking at me. There's a perfect image of Russian art: ox eyes bobbing in the soup. Or I'm walking in a field of thick, sweet smelling grass, and I come upon the skeleton of a horse, bleached white, and I see windmills turning in the distance, and suddenly I know that God is coming to kill me. I can feel him in the wind. That's what a writer's life is like. Eating soup that looks back at you and waiting in a field for God to come and kill you.

(Pause.)

I've disappointed you. Well, if you want to be a writer get used to it.

A Russian Play

Don Nigro

Seriocomic
Radetsky, 33,

> *Radetsky is a doctor at a mental institution in the Russian provinces in the summer of 1900. His only pleasure is in visiting the Volkonsky estate, where Madame Volkonsky has three beautiful daughters: the exquisite Natasha, the serious and socially minded Katya, and the young and innocent Anya. Here he is explaining to his writer friend Nikolay, whom all women adore, what it's like to be an unsuccessful lover, how frustrating it is to be rejected, and how one is so desperate for love that one's love can move from one person to another in the blink of an eye. Radetsky is a good man who means well but drinks too much, feels too much, and is very unlucky in love. He has just come upon Nikolay kissing the innocent Anya.*

RADETSKY: Katya is a wonderful girl. Of course she hates me. All women hate me. And do you know why? Because I love them. If I hated them, they'd be falling all over me, like they do with you. That's why I hate women. I'm a complete fool. First I was desperately in love with Natasha. She's so beautiful. I thought I'd go mad if I didn't have her. And I think she might actually have loved me, as well, with a little encouragement. But then she let her mother persuade her to marry that simpleton Grigorayev, because she thought he had the money to save her precious estate, and in despair I began having long conversations with Katya about building a clinic for the peasants---not that I had any very strong philanthropic interests, but at least being with Katya was one step away from being with Natasha. It made me feel still connected to her, in some stupid way. And after a bit, I found that my affections were gradually moving from Natasha to Katya. We were together every day, when she came to help at the mental hospital She would talk so earnestly to me, with her face close to mine. How was I to know it was because she's incredibly nearsighted, and too vain to wear glasses? She smelled so good. But one day I try to kiss her and she acts as if I'd just drawn her a diagram of my penis. It was appalling, to see her reaction. So lately I've begun flirting with Anya, to try and make Katya jealous, and what happens? I walk out of the hedge-maze and find her whole head in your mouth. And the most ridiculous thing is, God help me, I think now I've begun to fall in love with Anya. But Anya, of course, is in love with you. But you don't really want her because you're in love with Natasha, who I don't want any more. My conclusion is that all men are vermin, and should be killed. And, lucky for me, as a doctor, I'm in an excellent position to do something about that.

Seven Minutes in Heaven
Steven Levenson

Seriocomic
Derek, mid-teens

> *Derek is one of six high school freshmen at a Friday night party in Margot's basement. The night has officially been a washout for Derek, whose attempts to hook up with Margot have been sharply rebuffed. After Phoebe earlier outed Derek for drinking in the bathroom, he finally sees his chance for revenge.*

DEREK: I dare you to go upstairs. Go to the kitchen. If someone's in there, you just, you don't say anything, you just ignore them. If you say something, you lose. Find a jar of peanut butter and a jar of mayonnaise. If someone asks you something, if they ask you a question, you don't answer. You don't nod, you don't shake your head. Take the peanut butter, take the mayonnaise, find a bathroom. Close the door to the bathroom. First you take the peanut butter and you put it on your cheeks, in three vertical lines. One. Two. Three. Then take more peanut butter and rub it on your neck, so it covers your neck. Your whole neck, like a cast. I'm not done. Put the peanut butter down. Get the mayonnaise. Take the mayonnaise and make a moustache and a goatee out of it. They have to connect. Then make mutton chops. Make them thick. Then put three scoops of it in your hair, whatever way you want, but it has to be three scoops. Big scoops. Then wash your hands so you don't get it all over the doorknobs and the cabinets and everything. Open the bathroom door. Go back to the kitchen. Put the peanut butter and the mayonnaise back where you got them. If someone's in there, nothing, no words, no signals, nothing. Go to the front door. Open the front door. Walk to the end of the driveway. When you get to the mailbox, stop. Put your hands up behind your head, like someone's pointing a gun at you. Stay there. Like that. After five minutes someone will come and get you. They will lead you back to the house with your hands behind your back, like you're a prisoner. You won't say or do anything. You just walk. One step after the other. If you say anything, or if you laugh or if you cry or if you do anything at all, you lose. And if you lose, you have to put your face in the toilet that Wade pooped in underwater for thirty seconds with your eyes open. Those are the rules.

Still Life
Alexander Dinelaris

Dramatic
Jeff, 35-40

> *Jeff is a trend analyst, who has just found out that he may have cancer. On the very same day, he meets the woman who could very well change his life. Her name is Carrie Ann Daly, a famous photographer. In this scene, he has found his way to her apartment late at night. In the monologue, he tries to explain what he's doing there...*

JEFF: You don't know me. You don't know what you're getting yourself into. I don't know what you're getting yourself into. I might be-- (A Beat.) I just-- I had a scare the other day. I was almost hit by a bus. Just before I went to your show. And it forced me to thinking. About life. About how I've lived it so far. I don't know, I sat in a cab and paid the driver to keep circling the block. I was going to ask him to just drive me back home. But I didn't. Because it occurred to me, that I've lived my whole life as a coward. Completely selfish and completely afraid. So, I thought, if I could get out of the car. Just get out and walk into that gallery. It sounds ridiculous, but I thought, maybe I was there for a reason. Maybe there was something inside, something, somebody, and that was going to be a sign... Jesus Christ, I sound like a-- (A Beat.) It's the fucking creme de menthe. That's when I saw your pictures. And they were, I can't explain it, beautiful. And death didn't seem-- For that moment, I stopped being afraid. I mean I was pissed that you made dying seem so, I don't know, acceptable. But I wasn't afraid. That's why I walked up to you. You gotta believe me. I'm not the guy who-- But I did. And we talked, and it was like I was myself. Or at least the self I wanted to be, or should have been. It's a week now, talking to you every day, and that feeling hasn't gone away. And now I'm standing here, feeling like that, and I just-- I don't want to screw it up. (A Beat.) Does that make any sense?

Still Life
Alexander Dinelaris

Dramatic
Terry, 35-45

> *Terry is the owner of a very hot trend consultancy. He is a no-nonsense guy who says exactly what's on his mind. In this scene he has been talking, drinking and flirting with a younger girl named Lena for some time. As Terry cuts to the chase, Lena feigns shock and tries to make her exit. Terry puts her in her place as he goes in for the kill.*

TERRY: I apologize. It's just that I sat here and listened to you for almost an hour. I think the least you could do is listen to me for two minutes. I said, I think we should go home and fuck. Now, which part of that offended you? I mean, we've been sitting here drinking and flirting for an hour. You touched my arm four times and my neck once. You told me you didn't love your husband. You said, "I like my husband, I'm just not sure if I love him." I'm not judging. Frankly, I don't give a shit. But I say, "Let's fuck". And you get up in a huff. Why? Was it a surprise? I don't think so. So what's the reaction all about? I'll tell you what I think. I think you're so bored with your life, that when your husband goes away, you come out and you stick your feet in the water. You drink. You flirt. You feel like a sexy girl. And you are, believe me, a sexy girl. Then, when it gets too hot... or too late. You find a reason to make your exit. I said, "Let's fuck". And you had your out. What were you going to do then? Huh? Go home, get in the tub with your water massage shower head and fantasize about what the rest of the night would have been like? I'm saying you don't have to. I know you feel bad. I do, too. I know you feel dirty. I do, too. I know that for one night, you just want to have your hair pulled and your ass slapped. You want to be free. Just once. Without feeling self-conscious. Without feeling guilty. Without it being pretend. I'm saying you can have it. I'm normal I'm healthy. I won't hurt you... unless you want me too. Most of all, I won't call you in the morning. *(A Beat.)* I won't call you ever again. One night of freedom. One night of anything goes. One night that actually exceeds those high expectations of yours. One night. And then you can get back to that life you like so much. Now, I'm going to say it again. *(A Beat.)* I think we should go home and fuck.

They Float Up
Jacqueline Reingold

Dramatic
Darnell, 20s, African-American

> *Darnell is a New Orleans native. He is sitting in a side room away from the action at a Bourbon Street strip club, speaking to a woman who has introduced herself as "Jucee," 40s, a white woman from upstate New York. Jucee has lost her job Up North and has come to The Big Easy in hopes of landing a job as an "exotic dancer." So far, no luck. When Jucee, frustrated Darnell won't help her get a job as a topless dancer, insults Darnell, he challenges all of her assumptions.*

DARNELL: You don't know anything about me. You're some weird lady looking to have an adventure. What ever you think about me, this bar, this town, you made up. You watched it on TV. It was a good story, right? Everyone felt outraged. Everyone felt sad. And everyone gave money, right? I bet even you did. Everyone wanted to help. But what happened? It's four years later, and did it get better? Try leaving the Quarter. You been to t he places where the tourists ain't at? I'll give you a tour. Then tell me if it's better. You know how many homeless people we got? Mostly old, sick people, the lucky ones sleeping in abandoned buildings. The unlucky ones dying in the street. The government even tried t o take back the damn trailers. But you think it's over. History. Something that happened. Cause the restaurants are open. They're making TV shows here now. And the Saint s wont the Super Bowl.

Why, in a way, it helped get us a new president. Things must be better. If he's our president. Right? *(A Beat.)* Maybe you need glasses. Cause you're not seeing so good. You know what really happened here? Same thing happened everywhere. We just got hit first. It wasn't the storm, it wasn't the winds or the rain or the flood, it was a way of thinking, that's what killed people. It was greed, cause without that it woulda turned out different. So a few years later, it went everywhere. Like the water over the levees, an ocean of greed, spread all over the country, like God laughing at us, I swear, showing us what for. And who got the worst of it ? Whose faces do you still see on the TV, talking about the homes they lost , the jobs, the healthcare they still can't afford, the lives that are ruined: same ones, in this country, in Haiti, everywhere: poor, black, uneducated. And five years later - - everything's the same, only the water's turned into oil, mill ions of gallons pumping into the gulf, killing everything in its way. So you want t o come down here thinking this place is friendly, it's for fun, it'll make you f eel young, men are gonna want to throw money at you cause they'll see the hidden what ever they didn't know they had? You'll be lucky to get out alive. This is where it started.

Things of Dry Hours
Naomi Wallace

Dramatic
Corbin, mid to late 30s

> *Corbin Teel is a white, mid to late thirties, working class Iowan. Its the*
> *1930's. Corbin has just woken up in the house of a stranger. He has slept on*
> *the floor. Tice, his host, comes in with a bowl of cereal and eats breakfast,*
> *ignoring Corbin. Corbin is hungry and hopes he'll be fed. But first he needs*
> *to impress Tice with his story.*

ORBIN: I'd pay you board but I got no money. Had some. Not much. A drink.
A knuckle of bread. They say you're for the workin' man, colored and
white. Speakin' for the jobless, organizin' for work relief. That the Party's
the only place in Birmingham where men like me and you sit at the
same table. Where the colored man can speak against the white man if
he's done wrong, even kick him out the Party if he acts with disrespect.
No other place like that. Well I'm jobless now. I was loading coal at T
C I. Beside men like you. Never got high up. Before that, button cutter
in Muscatine. Iowa. That's where I was born. Cutting buttons from
Mississippi river mussel shells. You got a shirt with buttons. I might of
made one of those buttons. Ever been in a button cuttin' room? The
shells give off a fine white dust that don't settle. You walk out after your
shift and you're covered in it. Just like snow. Even in August. Forty men
coming off our shift at midnight like an army of snowmen. In the heat.
Hard times hit, they dumped our wages, over and over 'til the money
they put in my hand. Well. *(He holds his empty hand out)* Added up to
that. But I still hung on. Signed a yellow-dog contract, fixed rate, said
yes to no union. But we got laid off anyhow. Then on down here to
Alabama. Second day in the mines a man next to me puts his pickax in
my thigh right to the bone. That's where I got my limp. But I never lost
a day of work in that mine. 'Til they laid us off. You ever hear a pickax
hit the bone? *(Makes a sound of the pick in the bone)* There's some of us,
they work. Others of us, they look like they work. Can't hardly tell the
difference. But I can.

Things of Dry Hours
Naomi Wallace

Dramatic
Tice Hogan, 50s, African-American.

1930's. Alabama. In this scene Tice speaks to the audience. Tice is sharpening a small piece of steel, a home-made blade, while he speaks.

TICE: You ever had a knife at your throat? It's overrated. A knife at my throat I can see doesn't bother me the way the ones I can't see, do. 'Cause most of us have got the ones we can't see circling 'round our neck and all your life you've got to watch which way you turn your head or you'll get. Stuck. *(He holds out the knife.)* Here, how sharp it is? Feel it. See how it shines? *(Now he withdraws the real knife and slowly holds out his other hand with the invisible knife in it.)* And this one, the one you can't see, feel that blade. Go on. Touch it. Just touch it. *(Beat)* There's nothing like it. *(Suddenly he throws the invisible knife high up into the air above him. He does some wild dodges and then catches the invisible knife in the air, perfectly.)* Damn I like that one. One of my soap box favourites: the invisible knife. And this takes me back to ...apples. Over the years, it started to rub on me, how I used the apple. The fruits of labor, the apple tree family. Etceteras. But then I got to thinkin' 'bout the apple and yeah, its flesh is white, with all these little black seeds inside and I thought hmmm. Follow it a little further and the good part, the sweet part is the white flesh. Who cares about those little black seeds? You eat one by mistake, you just *(does three quick spits)*. Not a second thought. So I quit on the apples. Gave them a rest for a while. But it creeps up on me, because the seeds are, naturally, at the core; the seed is the core. You swallow one, it shoots right back out, ready to make a tree wherever it lands. *(Says the following in one, smooth breath:)* And then it comes to me a little further that maybe an apple is just an apple for a horse not a man and better left out of conversation all together. Things fall apart, yeah. They do. With time. But what's the reason and what's the rhyme?

Tigers Be Still
Kim Rosenstock

Dramatic
Zack, late teens.

Zach has been very disturbed since his mother died. He has decided to leave home and here, in direct address to the audience, he tells us what he was thinking when he made that decision.

ZACK: This is how it happens. I wait until my dad has gone into his room for the night and then I grab the suitcase that's been sitting under my bed, packed, for months.

Then I go to the kitchen to grab a box of cookies and leaning up against the leg of the table I see the rifle. And for the first time it hits me: My dad has a rifle. And that's not ok. He needs someone to take it away. So I do that. I walk out of the house I've lived in my whole life with a rifle, most of my belongings and a box of cookies and I have no idea if I have the courage to go any further than the town pond, which is where I'm standing, looking at the ducks when I hear it: a soft rumbling, a growling.

And I turn around. And there it is. The tiger. At the town pond. And I'm, like, armed, you know. And I think—I can be the guy who defended the town from the tiger. And I'm about to pull the trigger when everything just becomes really, really still. I stare into the tiger's big, yellow eyes and I swear it's like he wants me to shoot him. He's tired. And alone. And lost. And I think: yeah, sure this tiger's dangerous—but like if you really think about it, who isn't? And he squints and stares at me in this sad, broken way and in that moment, for him, I choose life.

I slowly lower the gun and as I do the tiger glares at me like "Oh great. Thanks for nothing, asshole." And he just turns around and walks away.

So then I'm just standing there, thinking to myself, "Now what?" When suddenly I drop the rifle and it goes off at my feet and at the sound of the gunshot I run—I run as fast I can, suitcase and everything. I run until I'm at the bus station and then I get on a bus and then I get on another bus. And that's how I escape.

Time Stands Still
Donald Margulies

Dramatic
James, mid to late 30s

James is talking to Sarah, the woman he lives with. He is a journalist; she is a photographer. Sarah has recently returned from Iraq, where she was badly injured by a roadside by a roadside bomb. Here, James tries to persuade Sarah that maybe it's time for both of them to live a more comfortable, safe life.

JAMES: Hey. *(Pause.)* We don't have to do this anymore, you know. We don't have to do this. We can stay home. We can make a home.

(A Beat.)

Y'know? The past few months? Teaching myself how to cook, watching Netflix... writing while you napped, listening to you breathe... I've been so... *(Chokes up)* happy. Y'know? Simple, boring, happy.

(A Beat.)

For the first time in I don't know how long, I don't have giardia, or some nasty parasite I'm trying to get rid of... And my back doesn't ache from sleeping on the ground, or on lousy mattresses in shitty hotels. I realized: Wow, this is what it must feel like to be comfortable. I don't think I've ever known that feeling; maybe as a boy I did, I felt safe, but I didn't know what it was. Now I know! I just want to be comfortable! There! I said it! Does that make me a bad person? I've been feeling like, We're going back there? Why? Unfinished business? Fuck unfinished business. I don't need to dodge bullets to feel alive anymore. Or step over mutilated corpses. Or watch children die. I want to watch children grow. And take vacations like other people. To... I don't know, dude ranches. Or Club Med. I don't want to be on a goddamn mission every time I get on a plane! I want to take our kids to Disney World and buy them all the crap they want. Let's just do it. We keep putting it off, and putting it off. We're pushing our luck already. Let's just go ahead and do it. Now. Not six months from now.

(Pause.)

There'll always be something, some reason to put our lives on hold. The war du jour. Well, fuck it. It's our turn now. (A Beat.) Let's stop running.

Trust
Paul Weitz

Dramatic
Morton, 30s

>   *Morton is laying into his girlfriend, a professional dominatrix, who has threatened to throw him out.*

MORTON: SHUT THE FUCK UP. Don't EVER tell me to get out of my own place. You hear me? Not ever. You harlot. You cunt. I found this place. I let you stay here when you were kicked out of your place. You were gonna live on the street. Worse, you were going to go home. You were gonna go back to your pathetic, zombie mother. I saved you from that. I saved you from Westchester. Who do you think you're talking to? You think you're talking to one of your customers? One of those pussies? Those fat fruits who miss getting spanked by their mommies? You can't play that game with me. You're tough with those pussies, but it's an act. I know that. It's an act. Come on. Don't make me the villain here. Come on. You love me. You know you love me. Who else knows you? Nobody else knows you. And nobody else loves you. Nobody could love you like I do. I love you more than anything. I love you more than my own vocabulary. Nobody else could love you like I do.

Trust
Paul Weitz

Morton, 30s

Morton is laying into his girlfriend, a professional dominatrix, who has threatened to throw him out. She has recently re-connected with a high school friend who came to her for a "session," who is extremely wealthy.

MORTON: What if I did get a real job? Would you quit? No, you wouldn't. You LIKE things like this. You LIKE CONTROLLING PEOPLE. You like ME like this. If I suddenly became normal, a normal fuck like everyone else out there, like those bugs? You'd dump me! You'd be out of that door! This is YOUR FAULT. I wasn't always like this! I GOT 1560 ON MY S.A.T.'S! I SHOULD BE THE ONE WITH A HUNDRED MILLION DOLLARS! WHERE'S MY MONEY? WHERE'S MY FUCKING MONEY? Jesus, my balls just got sucked up into my stomach. you know what you just reminded me of? My mother. The way she used to nag my father, get a job, get a real job, until he broke down and sold insurance. He sold accidental death and dismemberment insurance, until his soul accidentally died and got dismembered. Get a job? Doing what? What should I be? A dog-groomer? A fireman? A research scientist? You know how FUCKING BORING it is to be in a lab ten hours a day? Standing on the shoulders of giants? You know who stands on the shoulders of giants? MIDGETS. Alright. I won't talk to him again. Scout's honor. Can I watch the end of the game now, if it's not already over? You love me. Don't forget that.

The Tyranny of Clarity
Brian Dykstra

Dramatic
Muddkat, could be any age

> *Muddkat speaks like jazz, trying to talk his friend (Big Papa B) into retiring from competition. Big Papa B is the world slam champion poet and is challenged by Double D to one last slam battle. Muddkat needs to be sure Big Papa B understands what happens to his legacy if he battles and loses.*

MUDDKAT: Okay. ...Every fighter wants to be Rocky Marciano. Even if they don't know it. Everybody. Nobody can. I did. I wanted to be him. 49 and 0. Retire undefeated. Heavyweight champion of the world. This is back when there was only one heavyweight champion of the world, only one per weight class. Not like now. Alphabet soup Eastern Bloc champions you can't name on Jeopardy. But, back then, hell there was only one real champ. Lightweights, welterweights, middleweights, they're all at least one rung down the ladder. There was only one heavyweight. Only one king. "Baddest Man On The Planet." Right? Can only be one of those. And at the top of that ladder of heavyweight champs lives Rocky Marciano. 49 and 0. Oh, you might pick Muhammad Ali, sure. You might not. But, in a fight with both in their primes Ali might have taken chips of the old rock, might have sent him down, face first. You watch a fighter go down face first, they never beat the count. Never. Clip him going backwards and there's some of that power gets dissipated. A fighter lands on his ass and most of the time he's up by six, bouncing cobwebs out of his head. Catch him coming in? Step into your glove while a man's coming forward and his weight catches your leather but his forward motion isn't off balance enough so he keeps coming through every bit of that straight right, or worse, he leans into a hook, his brain sloshes forward, and he falls, face first, first thing to stop his fall is his broken nose. Think George Foreman in the eighth. He will not get up. That fight is over before he even hits the canvas. But Ali? No. He lost. First to Smokin' Joe Frazier's left hook, then four more times, including to some bum named Leon Spinks. No, Ali at his best might have been better, might have even been "The Greatest Of All Time! Float Like A Butterfly, Sting Like A Bee!" But even he, even he wants to be Rocky Marciano. Rocco Francis Marchegiano sold shoes. He did. In Brockton, Mass, for his father. But he couldn't cut it. So he showed up in a gym one day and started working with his hands. Crawled up out of poverty, and walked away with a perfect record. Perfect. You name me another heavyweight champ who did that with that many fights and you'll be making it up. But that's not what's so impressive. That's not the thing. I mean, can you imagine it? Can you imagine calling it quits? Can you? You are 49 and nothing. You are arguably more famous than the president. You are arguably the most famous man in the whole world. Who the hell was president back then? "I Like Ike," sure, but they Loved Rocky Marciano. And that number sits out there. It tempts you like sirens, like perfection, like your destiny whispering: ...Fifty... Fifty. Perfect. Half a hundred. Divisible by ten. Got that Zero in it. Five-O É and O. There it was. One. One More. One More Fight. For perfection...And he walked away. Where does that psychology come from? How are you going to leave that out there? How is anyone? 49 and 0? With perfection squared, on the table, one fight away? 49 and 0. How are you going to leave 50 on the table? And it wasn't like he was ducking nobody. Nobody really believes he couldn't have whipped Floyd Patterson, although Patterson had some game, or Ingemar Johansson. He coulda' beat Johansson, easy. Motherfucker up and walked away. I still don't know how he did it. I couldn't have. I might have ended up 49 and 1. Wrecked the whole masterpiece. But I woulda' had to take a shot at fifty, even if there was only a three percent chance of winning. Why didn't he? Why didn't he need it? They all come back. One more time, one more fight, once more in the spotlight, one more shot at glory. But nobody, nobody ever had a better reason for one more fight, than Rocky Marciano. And he stayed away. Wouldn't give the public what they wanted. Hell, wouldn't give the public what he wanted. He must have wanted it, right? How could he not? Or maybe that's the question. How could he not? But even so, even after not chasing fifty, everybody wants to be Rocky Marciano. I don't know how he did that. I don't know how he made 49 and 0 more perfect. Than fifty.

This

Melissa James Gibson

Tom, early 40's

Tom is addressing his wife's best friend in the hallway outside her apartment door.

TOM: I think about you Jane
You invade perfectly benign thoughts
all the time
I'll be buying bread trying to figure out the
optimal number of grains and there you
will be with your hand clasping the back
of your neck lost in thought
There you'll be standing with your hand on
your hip and your scrunched-up smile
and I'll think about how I want to
touch you
I watch you I've been watching you
for years and
I'm not stupid I know I'm going
through something and I
know it's partly adjusting to having a
child and nothing will be the same
and I know it's
partly the stress of my close-but-
never-a-cigar business and
it's also just this feeling that I'm the
guy who never gets in the door
never gets past the waiting area
and the chairs are uncomfortable in
the waiting area
and I don't know what I'm saying
except that I feel the only thing
that gives me any pleasure lately
and I know this is a terrible thing to say
especially because Marrell and I have
just been given the gift of this boy but

the only thing that gives me any pleasure
is the thought of touching you Jane
some day and
sometimes I hear
these voiceovers in my head narrating
my life and it's true that sometimes
the voice just sounds like bad
advertising copy but sometimes the
voice says things that feel very
compelling and that voice
has started narrating some things I'm
finding very very hard to resist
and the other thing I think about as I
think about touching you is that I've
thought about touching you for so
long and forgive me for saying this
but when Roy
when Roy died
and I know this is shameful but when
he died I thought
Oh maybe it could be me now Maybe
I could
and I know I know
I'm sorry
but Jane there's a small part of me that
always wondered what if
what if
(An actual proposition) What If Jane

We Are Here

Tracy Thorne

Seriocomic
Eli, 13

Eli is speaking to his mother, Billie. In reality, Eli is dead. Billie imagines speaking to him throughout the play. In this scene, Billie is distraught and Eli is trying to cheer her up.

ELI: Here's what we do. I be, like, a secret agent, yo. Who just saved the USA from bein' invaded by the bad army soldiers who don't want us to have our freedom, right? I be, like, the brother who makes sure America stays free forever! BY BLOWING STUFF UP, YO!

(Eli makes a huge, explosive sound effect, as only teenage boys can.)

And then I'll bust a move in my tricked out ride that the evil doers CANNOT capture cause it's so gadgety, check! Batman and Bond be scared to start my engine, "Ooooo, he's too bad and we're too old!" Yes mam, I'm a smooth new brother, those Action Jacks got nothing on me. I make sure everysinglebody feels safe all day long. How do I do this, you may ask? Cause I look awesome in my leather, check! And I own a hundred pairs 'a shiny kicks, don't I? Hey, ain't no comfort like when Dad's in the house. And you, gorgeous, you could be like my boss, yo. In a suit. A Italian lady suit. Sweet. And we could be having one 'a those adult type, smooth and quiet, victory cocktails, la la la. You know, before, we be doin' explosions all over the place, you wearing the headset giving the word, me doin' noise and mayhem, car crashes, the lot. Snap! And after, we be two suave grown ups who maybe slide onto a big leather sofa with a kind of, 'we knew it all along' type nerve. And the drinks'll be mixed ones, the kind you shake, psych! But since this is pretending, mine'll be really 7UP so you, Billie you, don't have to worry that I, Eli I, will get drunk or nothin'. And then you'll be happy. Cause I'm the brother who saved the day. Let's pretend that.

We Are Here

Tracy Thorne

Dramatic
Hal, 30

Hal is speaking to his sister-in-law, Shawn. It is the evening before his wife and newborn son come home from the hospital Hal and Shawn have been celebrating with tequila and are feeling no pain. Hal is a contractor who builds subsidized housing. His wife has a talent for happiness that he could never understand–until perhaps now. Shawn, even with her self proclaimed "bottomless longing," has worked hard for her own happiness. The screaming he refers to happened when he announced his wife was pregnant.

HAL: Hey, I'll admit it. I humor her. Play along...she's the love of my life, what else am I gonna do? And then she's having a baby, my baby, so I'm completely terrified of that, but I have to pretend I'm not terrified or she'll ratchet up the whole 'joy of life' nightmare to such an extent that it becomes an actual nightmare, well more of one, so there's this whole hidden component, because if she knew the true extent of my crap world view she might decide I'm not worth the trouble, and her having decided--SO DECISIVELY--that I am worth the trouble was the thing that introduced the idea of hope to me in the first place because I was, by necessity, completely hopeless! My entire life's work constructed to disguise the extent of my hopelessness. Building building after building for all the worthy people as an antidote to hopelessness. Which is an inevitable failure because how could you be anything but hopeless in this universally hopeless life! UNLESS, you've been drinking whatever Kool Aide the Nash's put in their morning coffee to put a song in your heart! I mean even YOU! Dim-world-view you! You have a song in your heart, bottomless longing notwithstanding! You gotta be hopeful and filled with some other brand of stubborn promise to teach Latin to thirteen year olds! To have it occur to you to teach Latin to thirteen year olds! Shit storm almighty, to even study Latin long enough to be qualified to teach Latin! Fuck Latin, I saw you! With Billie and your mother! That night! The three of you screaming! I mean what the fuck was that?! I, under no circumstances known to man, would be capable of that. Even your father, who has got to be one of the most satisfied, fortunate, DELIGHTED guys in the world, admitted he was incapable of that. Making a joyful noise such as that. YOU can do that, Shawn. 'Bottomless longing you' can do that. How the fuck do you do that? Except now, maybe I know. Maybe nothing, I DO know! No equivocation whatsoever and it's a criminal offense Billie Nash is not here to see this. NOW, I KNOW!! Let the blessed universe suck on that!

SCENES

A Bright New Boise
Samuel D. Hunter

Dramatic
Will, late 30s

> *Leroy, early to mid-20s Will, a disgraced evangelical from Northern Idaho,
> has left his former life and moved to Boise in order to reconnect with his son
> Alex, whom he hasn't seen in 17 years. In an awkward attempt to get closer
> to him, he gets a job at the local Hobby Lobby, where Alex has a summer
> job. Unbeknownst to Will, Leroy—a co-worker—has a stake in keeping Alex
> away from him.*

> *Later that day. LEROY sits in the break room reading a newspaper, wearing
> a T-shirt that reads simply "FUCK" in large block letters. Hobby Lobby TV
> plays in the background. After a moment, WILL enters with some lunch in a
> Tupperware container. He notices LEROY's shirt, and nods politely at him.
> WILL goes to the microwave, puts in his lunch, and turns it on.*

LEROY: It's a piece of shit.
WILL: *(turning)*
    What's that?
LEROY: The microwave. It barely works, I'd recommend cranking it up to high
    and leaving it in there for at least three times longer than normAL:
WILL: Oh—okay, thanks.
    WILL turns the microwave up.
LEROY: How's the first day?
WILL: Second, actually. Well, first full day. It's—fine. Slow.
LEROY: It's always like this. You'd think they were losing money, but the profit
    margin is pretty amazing.
WILL: What do you mean?
LEROY: Think about it. They're just selling all this raw material; fabric, paint,
    balsa wood, whatever. It's like the customers are paying money to do the
    manufacturing process themselves. You know those foam balls, the ones
    we sell for ninety-nine cents, the one the size of a baseball?
WILL: Yeah.
LEROY: Those things cost less than a penny to make.
WILL: Is that right?
LEROY: That's right.

WILL: Wow. Highway robbery.

LEROY: What?

WILL: Oh, I just—that's a big markup.

LEROY: You think it's dishonest?

WILL: Oh, I—I didn't mean that—

LEROY: You didn't?

WILL: No, I was just... It was just a joke.

> *(Pause.)*

LEROY: I'm deliberately making you uncomfortable.

> Awkward *(Pause.)* WILL turns off the microwave and takes out his lunch. He sits at a table across the room from LEROY and begins to eat.LEROY grabs his newspaper and sits down next to WILL.

LEROY: *(extending a hand)*

> Leroy.

WILL: Oh, it's—

LEROY: Will. I know.

WILL: How do you know my—?

> LEROY points to his nametag.

WILL: Oh. Heh.

> *(pointing to Leroy's shirt)*

> So do you—? You actually wear that to work?

LEROY: For as long as I can before Pauline sees me.

WILL: You don't get in trouble?

LEROY: I'm the only one in this store who knows anything about art supplies, so I can basically do whatever I want. I'm the only one that can answer actual questions.

WILL: Are you an artist?

LEROY: Getting my masters in Fine Arts at BSU.

WILL: What kind of art to you make?

LEROY: points to his t-shirt.

WILL: I—don't understand—

LEROY: I also have one that says "cunt", one that says "you will eat your children", and one that has a color photograph of my penis on both sides.

WILL: Oh.

LEROY: I'm forcing people to confront words and images they normally avoid. Especially at a place like this.

WILL: You—you mean the Hobby Lobby?

LEROY: Exactly. It's about the interaction between the word and the kinds of people who shop here, deliberately making them uncomfortable. Soccer m oms and grade school kids and little old ladies, they all have to confront the reality of the words before they get their arts and crafts supplies. You want a foam ball? FUCK. You want some acrylic paints? CUNT. You want some pipe cleaners? YOU WILL EAT YOUR CHILDREN. It's the only reason I work here, I could have got some boring job on campus just as easy. But where's the art in that?

(Pause.)

WILL: Well I'm just gonna finish up my—

LEROY: You just move to town?

WILL: Um. Yes, actually.

LEROY: Where from?

WILL: Up north.

LEROY: Where up north?

WILL: Outside of Couer d'Alene.

LEROY: Where outside of Couer d'Alene?

WILL: Um. Small town.

LEROY: Beautiful up there.

WILL: Yes, it is, it's really— Have you spent time up there?

LEROY: Little bit. Family trips, you know. Things like that. Kootenai county, right?

WILL: That's right.

LEROY: Rathdrum—that's around there, isn't it?

(Pause.)

WILL: Yeah, that's actually—well, I grew up in Rathdrum.

LEROY: Is that right? Pretty small town, right?

WILL: Pretty small.

LEROY: Must be hard to be in Boise after such a nice little quiet town like that, huh?

WILL: Boise's actually / very nice—

LEROY: What was the name of that church up in Rathdrum? The one that was in the papers a few months ago—Life Church, New Order—?

WILL: New Life Fellowship.

LEROY: Right, New Life. I kind of last track of the story after a while—is your pastor in jail yet, or is he still awaiting trial?

(Pause.)

You see this? This is me deliberately making you uncomfortable. This is your "FUCK" t-shirt.

(Pause.)

WILL: Well, I figured this would happen.

LEROY: I actually think this is kind of cool, it's like I'm talking to a survivor of Jonestown or something.

WILL: Is there a reason that you're doing this?

LEROY: Alex is my little brother. Adopted brother, whatever.

(Pause.)

WILL: I know how this looks. And you're right to be defensive but—honestly, after what happened, I'm just trying to start again.

LEROY: You still believe in all that?

WILL: I still believe in God.

LEROY: What about the other stuff? All that crazy crap your pastor was preaching about, you still believe in all that?

(Pause.)

WILL: I don't know.

(Pause.)

I'm trying to leave all that behind.

(Pause.)

LEROY: Okay, look. I read through some of the articles last night. From what I can tell, you didn't have anything to do with that kid who died. And I get that you coming down here is just your ham-fisted attempt to put your life on a new track. But you're going about this in the creepiest way possible, confronting him at work like this.

WILL: I didn't know what else to do, I was worried your parents wouldn't allow me to see him—

LEROY: Yeah, well, John and Cindy drink enough nowadays that they probably wouldn't even care that you're here. But believe me, I care.

(Pause.)

Just stay away from him, okay? Don't fuck with him. Don't try to "convert" him or whatever.

WILL: I won't. I don't do that anymore.

Darkpool
Don Nigro

Seriocomic
Dutch, 37
Mick, 29

Dutch and Mick are operatives in the employ of Darkpool Associates, a mysterious and rather sinister company which has been contracted by the government to engage in a variety of somewhat shady tasks in support of a larger military operation in an unspecified foreign country. They have been called back to corporate headquarters after being involved in an incident in which a number of perhaps innocent residents of this foreign country have been gunned down in a village square. The previous day they've met with Max, the head of Darkpool, a Christian fundamentalist who believes his company can take over the world, and Justine, a young lawyer and public relations expert, whose job it will be to handle the situation in a way that protects the company. Dutch is a veteran operative, tough and cynicAL: Mick is an Ohio farm boy who joined up to have adventures. Justine, worried that Mick will crack under pressure, has invited him to dinner at her apartment in the Darkpool complex and Mick has spent the night there. The next morning he encounters his Dutch at breakfast. Dutch and Mick are good friends and have been through a lot together, but they are very different people. Dutch is eating breakfast at a table. Mick appears.

(Morning. Dutch eating breakfast at a table. Mick appears.)
DUTCH: Hey there, sailor. Big night, huh?
MICK: It was good. It was good for me. I'm calmer now.
DUTCH: I'll bet you are.
MICK: What does that mean?
DUTCH: That girl knows how to relax a person, I'm sure. They taught her that in law school.
MICK: Nothing like that happened.
DUTCH: Okay.
MICK: We stayed up talking on the balcony until late. Then I fell asleep.
DUTCH: Uh huh.
MICK: She held my hand.
DUTCH: That's all she held?
MICK: It wasn't anything sexual

DUTCH: I see.

MICK: It was nice. It was the sort of company I needed.

DUTCH: I got you.

MICK: No. I don't think you do.

DUTCH: No, I've got you, all right.

MICK: She's not like she seems. I mean, she's warmer. She's a real person. She listens. And she's—it was good. It was more like, I don't know, tender. And innocent. That's what I needed. She could tell. Not sex. But a kind of closeness. I mean, there was a time or two, when she started asking me these questions, when I got upset. It made me uneasy. But I know she's just trying to help.

DUTCH: Just business.

MICK: No. Not just business. We made a real connection.

DUTCH: A connection.

MICK: Yes. Is that so hard for you to believe?

DUTCH: You know what she's doing, don't you? She's keeping you in the fold.

MICK: In the fold?

DUTCH: That's her job.

MICK: I don't know what you're talking about.

DUTCH: They're worried you're going to crack under pressure, so she gets cozy with you. You calm down a little. They get a better sense of what you're made of. And it makes it less likely that you'll leave the fold.

MICK: Leave the fold?

DUTCH: Spill the beans. Talk to the press. Say things that could hurt the company. She's in the fold. You want to be where she is. So you stay in the fold.

MICK: She's not like that.

DUTCH: Okay.

MICK: She's not like that, Dutch.

DUTCH: Fine. I'm not saying don't enjoy it. Life is short. Just watch your back, is all.

MICK: She's not that sort of person.

DUTCH: You ever have a girl like that before, Mick? A girl that good looking, that smart? Any girl like that ever show any interest in you before?

MICK: I've had plenty of girls.

DUTCH: Sure. Cute girls. Nice girls. Small town girls. Nobody like that one. Listen, kid. I don't want to spoil the moment for you, but you need to keep in mind that a woman is not a supernatural entity. A woman is a human being, and human beings are animals who'll stab you in the back, rip off your head and eat you if they get hungry enough. That's not a female characteristic, it's a human characteristic. The only kind of woman who's not that sort of person is an inflatable woman.

MICK: I don't want you talking about her like that.

DUTCH: Fine.

MICK: I mean it, Dutch.

DUTCH: What did you tell her?

MICK: I told her the truth.

DUTCH: And what did she say about it? Was she fine with that?

MICK: Yes.

> (Pause.)

She said we might want to tweak it a little.

DUTCH: Tweak it.

MICK: Just to make sure people understood.

DUTCH: Just to be sure nobody got the wrong idea.

MICK: Yes.

DUTCH: Uh huh.

MICK: What?

DUTCH: Spin. She wants to control the spin. Yes?

MICK: Something like that. She's going to help us.

DUTCH: Oh, me too? She's going to help me, too, is she? Well, that's all right then.

MICK: What's all right?

DUTCH: The first thing you do is separate the prisoners.

MICK: What are you talking about?

DUTCH: Nothing. I'm glad you had a good night. Sit down and have some eggs.

MICK: I've already eaten.

DUTCH: Yeah.

MICK: Dutch. I need this. Don't take it from me.

DUTCH: Okay.

MICK: I mean it.

DUTCH: Okay. Have some eggs.

Darkpool
Don Nigro

Seriocomic
Dutch, 37
Mick, 29

Dutch and Mick are operatives in the employ of Darkpool Associates, a mysterious and rather sinister company which has been contracted by the government to engage in a variety of somewhat shady tasks in support of a larger military operation in an unspecified foreign country. They have been called back to corporate headquarters after being involved in an incident in which a number of perhaps innocent residents of this foreign country have been gunned down in a village square. They've met with Max, the head of Darkpool, a Christian fundamentalist who believes his company can take over the world, and Justine, a young lawyer and public relations expert, whose job it will be to handle the situation in a way that protects the company. Dutch is a veteran operative, tough and cynicAL: Mick is an Ohio farm boy who joined up to have adventures. Justine, worried that Mick will crack under pressure, has been cultivating a relationship with him, which Mick believes is genuine, but Dutch thinks is just a tactic to keep him in line. Dutch has confronted Justine about this, insulted her, been slapped by her, and then kissed her, the last seen by Mick, who has walked out in anger. Max then tells Dutch he thinks Mick is going to do something stupid like tell the truth about what happened, and strongly implies that Dutch should push him off the garden rooftop so they could call it a suicide. Then he suggests that if Dutch doesn't cooperate, something unfortunate might happen to Dutch's daughter, the only person in the world besides his friend Mick that Dutch cares about. Dutch finds Mick on the rooftop garden that night, and both have to decide what to do. Mick has told Justine earlier that ever since he fell out of a barn and hit his head on a rusty pump, now and then, especially in times of danger, he can hear bees.

(Night. The rooftop garden. Mick and Dutch.)

MICK: So where the hell have you been? You been talking to that guy all this time?

DUTCH: I took a walk.

MICK: You took a walk outside?

DUTCH: I took a walk in the building.

MICK: You took a walk in the building?

DUTCH: I just started walking up and down corridors and in and out of rooms. I just needed to think.

MICK: I can see where talking to that guy would really mess up your head. I don't know how you can talk to that guy. That guy is certifiable. And he runs this huge corporation. And we work for him. How does that happen?

DUTCH: I don't know.

MICK: I just want to go somewhere quiet and live a quiet life. When I was a kid, I had this desperate longing for adventures, you know? I couldn't wait to get out into the world have all kinds of adventures. You know what I mean?

DUTCH: Yeah.

MICK: But this job has cured me of that. I am officially done with adventures. What I have learned from this job is that basically, adventures really suck, Dutch.

DUTCH: This is true.

MICK: And I kind of hope, I mean, maybe this is completely nuts, but I still kind of hope that maybe if I could get Justine away from all this crap, to someplace nice and quiet, we could maybe have some sort of a decent life, you know? Just settle down and have a couple of kids and be decent to people. She could still be a lawyer. I could fix cars or something. We could forget about all this.
(Pause.)
What? You think I'm crazy?

DUTCH: Kind of.

MICK: You really think she's just using me?

DUTCH: I don't know what she's doing, Mick. Maybe she don't either.

MICK: A person's got to have some hope, you know?

DUTCH: I guess.

MICK: A person's got to have the ability to believe in other people, at least some other people, maybe even just one other person, trust just one other person, at least, in their life. I mean, if you don't believe in anybody, what have you got?

DUTCH: I don't know.
(Pause.)

MICK: Why did you kiss her, Dutch?

DUTCH: I don't know. Maybe I was jealous. I'm sorry.

MICK: She didn't want to kiss you, did she?

DUTCH: No.

MICK: There are nice girls in the world, you know, Dutch.

DUTCH: I know.

MICK: You've known some nice girls, haven't you, Dutch?

DUTCH: Sure.

> *(Pause.)*

MICK: Dutch.

DUTCH: What?

MICK: I think we should tell the truth.

DUTCH: You think so?

MICK: I think so.

DUTCH: And what is the truth, Mick?

MICK: The truth is, we killed a lot of people for no reason.

DUTCH: Why did we do that, Mick?

MICK: I don't know. I was scared. That's why I did it. I was scared out of my mind, and I just wanted them all to get the hell away from me. But why should they do that? I mean, it was their road. It was their city. Why should they have to get the hell away from me? Why shouldn't I have to get away from them? Why did you do it, Dutch?

DUTCH: Shoot first. Motto of the living. Stop and talk. Motto of the dead.

MICK: But we shouldn't even have been there. We were supposed to go to some village or something, weren't we? But you decided to turn around and go back, and that's how we got lost in the first place. Why didn't we just do what we were told, Dutch?

DUTCH: It just didn't feel right.

MICK: What were we supposed to do in that village, anyway?

DUTCH: Sometimes you try to do the right thing, you just end up making everything worse.

> *(Pause.)*

MICK: So you don't think we should tell the truth?

> *(Pause.)*
>
> Dutch?

DUTCH: Half the time I don't know what the truth is, Mick.

MICK: Truth is your best honest guess at the time.

DUTCH: So your truth and my truth could be entirely different things.

MICK: I'm only responsible for mine, Dutch.

DUTCH: Mick, if you tell the truth, I think we're going to prison.

MICK: Maybe.

DUTCH: And how are you going to take Justine home to Ohio if you're in prison?

MICK: Maybe she'll wait for me.

DUTCH: Who's going to wait for me, Mick?

MICK: I don't know, Dutch. One of your ex-wives? One of your kids? A son or a daughter? Somebody like that? You have kids, don't you?

DUTCH: I have a daughter.

MICK: There you go.

DUTCH: There I go.

MICK: She'll wait for you.

DUTCH: You think?

MICK: Sure.

DUTCH: I don't know.

MICK: Sure she will. She's your daughter. She'd do anything for you. And you'd do anything for her. Because deep down, people are good. People love each other. You love your daughter, right, Dutch?

DUTCH: I never see her. But once in a while I get a picture. She's really beautiful. And smart. She's so smart. I'm putting her through college, Mick. That's what I'm doing with my money. She's going to Princeton.

MICK: That's great, Dutch.

DUTCH: But I can't do that from prison, Mick.

MICK: Yeah.
    (Pause.)
    So you think we should lie?

DUTCH: What's a lie, Mick?

MICK: You know what a lie is, Dutch. You might not know for sure what truth is, but a lie you can smell.
    (Pause.)
    I'm going to tell the truth. I don't care what that crazy fucker says. I'm going to tell the truth. That's how I was raised, and that's what I'm going to do.
    (Pause.)
    I hope you understand. I don't want to put you in a tight spot or anything.

DUTCH: I know that, Mick.

MICK: I just need to do this.

DUTCH: Uh huh.

MICK: Sometimes a person's got to do things they don't want to do. Isn't that right?

DUTCH: That's right.
    ((Pause.) Mick looks at Dutch, then goes over to look over the side.)

MICK: It sure is a long ways up here.

DUTCH: Yes it is.

MICK: And a long ways down.

(Pause.)

Did you hear that?

DUTCH: What?

MICK: It's so odd.

DUTCH: What is?

MICK: Bees. I thought I heard bees.

(Dutch looks at Mick. The light fades on them and goes out.)

The Dew Point

Neena Beber

Seriocomic
Kai, 20s
Jack, 20s

> *In this scene Kai, newly engaged to Mimi, debates the merits of monogamy with Jack, a confirmed womanizer who also happens to be Mimi's ex-boyfriend.*

(A bar. Jack and Kai each nurse drinks, go through legal papers.)

JACK: Thanks for helping me out.

KAI: No problem. Mimi asked me to, so I need for you to explain a few points—

JACK: Lay it on me.

KAI: What's Visqueen?

JACK: That's a popular vapor barrier.

KAI: Which is?

JACK: You want that on the warm side of a wall to prevent air from migrating through to the cool side and condensing.

KAI: Otherwise? I'm sure we studied this in high school, but I've cleared out those brain cells.

JACK: See, buildings used to be more loosely built. Masonry, that allows for air flow. Now air migrates through the wall, gets trapped in there and reaches its dew point inside the wall. This causes rot. So we need to create moisture and vapor barriers to stop the transpiration of warm moist air. You follow?

KAI: Otherwise air turns to moisture right inside the wall.

JACK: You could say that, yes. If it reaches its dew point – the temperature and pressure at which vapor condenses into liquid. You know, like on this glass.
(holding up his glass)
The moisture in the air is coming into contact with this cold glass and condensing. Warmer air can hold more moisture, and then when you introduce a cold surface, wham, when the air hits a certain temperature against the glass, the vapor condenses to water.

KAI: That's how we get dew?

JACK: When the air warms up more quickly than the earth, right. You see they had that kitchen, all the heat-generating equipment in that kitchen, right up against the refrigerated side of the bar, with no insulation in between.

KAI: And you didn't check this—

JACK: I wouldn't. I was brought in to do a very specific task. I happen to know about this stuff, but I don't need to.

KAI: Right. I am surprised you don't carry insurance.

JACK: I design furniture. I don't build buildings. The contractor is the one who oversees all this. I don't think that woman really broke her foot.

KAI: Probably looking for a settlement.

JACK: I don't think I personally should have to pay anything.

KAI: We should be able to get you out of this. It's not my area, but I have a colleague … I'll put you in touch with the right person.

JACK: I want to pay for all this, of course. For your time, too.

KAI: That won't be necessary.

JACK: At least let me buy the drinks.

(Kai shrugs "okay"; off his glass:)

KAI: I don't think I've ever much thought about where the moisture on a glass comes from. In the air all the time, all the time; that's interesting.

JACK: Everything is volatile.

KAI: It seems so.

JACK: Certain triggers—certain triggers and environmental conditions, they make visible, make

manifest what's already there. Take that waitress – that is a gorgeous woman, is she not?

KAI: I'd have to agree with you there.

JACK: And maybe I'm in a relationship, and maybe I think it's a good, stable thing, but then there is the introduction of this other being, and a once stable thing is rendered unstable. A question mark of possibility arises.

KAI: How's it going with Phyllis, Jack?

JACK: Phyllis is great. Phyllis is a phenomenal person.

KAI: I've always liked her very much.

JACK: But already, already I'm constantly defending myself. This bubble of suspicion I'm under-- Does Mimi question everything you do?

KAI: I try not to give her cause.

JACK: A relationship should not be mutual self-defense. And Phil, Phil can't admit to herself that the reason she's stayed single so long is because she's really much happier on her own.

KAI: I don't get that impression.

JACK: I think she's afraid of making the sacrifices, the compromises it takes. If she would admit that to herself, she'd be a much happier person.

KAI: Maybe she just hasn't met her match yet.

JACK: I'm not saying it can't work out with us. It can. It might. I hope it will. I really like her enormously.

KAI: Then make it work out, Jack. It may well be within your power to do so.

JACK: Now I'm looking at our waitress friend over there, I'm watching this other person, this stranger, and I want to know what her tits look like. I just want to know. Is that wrong?

KAI: I used to be like that. Undressed almost every women I saw—what would it be like—imagined that--

JACK: What happened?

KAI: I turned 16.

JACK: It's not just sexuAL: It may start there, but it's -- it's wanting to commune with another soul, to connect, to know this person wholly, totally-- Am I supposed to cut that off?

KAI: Not every itch has to be scratched, in my opinion. The feeling will pass. That urgency.

JACK: Half the people I know, men and women—and I'm not including you, Kai, but half of them, make that most of them, they're the walking dead. I won't become that. I don't think it's a natural thing, to be with one person for the rest of one's life – in the interest of what, safety? I don't believe in playing it safe. There's a biological reality we're fighting against.

KAI: And there's evolution.

JACK: Evolution?

KAI: I'd like to advance beyond my biological reality. Because you're right, there's fear – cutting ourselves off out of fear, out of conventionality – but if you want to talk about knowing a person wholly, totally – is that really what you're doing? There will always be more women, women who are interesting, and beautiful, and fascinating, and I won't get to be with all of them, but I will get further – and deeper – with the one beautiful and interesting and fascinating woman I've chosen. And I wouldn't do anything to hurt her. It's that simple.

JACK: Nice wedding toast, but you really think that's enough insulation?

KAI: Insulation?

JACK: You think that's enough insulation to keep those feelings contained? In the long run? When you're a little bored, and a little pissed off, let's say, and you miss certain feelings, and you think you might be able to get away with it …

KAI: If I knew I'd get away with shop lifting, I still wouldn't do it. Not to sound goody goody.

JACK: How about a hit of heroin? Guaranteed, absolute bliss, one time only, no consequences, guaranteed no consequences, would you try it?

KAI: It doesn't work that way, "no consequences." There's always a cost.

JACK: "Always a cost." I hate that way of thinking; okay then, there's also a cost to being bourgeois, conventional, complacent and comfortable.

KAI: You know what? I don't need to defend my desire for monogamy.

JACK: I'm sorry, I'm not trying to threaten you.

KAI: You're not. You know, Jack, I've been a newness junkie, too. I know what that's about. But even newness gets old after a while.

(Jack pauses, takes a sip of his drink.)

JACK: I like you, KAI:

(another beat)

I'm happy as shit for Mimi.

(Kai pauses, sipping his drink.)

KAI: I don't think of shit as happy.

(another beat)

JACK: That's funny.

KAI: *(of papers)*

Tell you what, I'll look these over. Connect you with the right person.

JACK: I'm grateful.

KAI: I'll call you if I have any more questions, but I'm hopeful we can make this go away.

JACK: That's great, Kai, I'm really—thanks. You know I want us to be friends. I'd love it if we could all be friends. Mimi's family to me. So I think of you—I'd like to think of you—at the very least as someone who doesn't actively dislike me.

KAI: I don't dislike you, Jack.

JACK: Then good.

KAI: I'd even go so far as to say I like you. Any resentment I have is not because of the current dynamic, but because you hurt Mimi. You cheated on her, and you lied to her, and you hurt her. And that angers me, it does, because I really can't stand thinking of Mimi getting hurt.

JACK: I understand. We hurt each other, in truth, but look, I understand.

KAI: *(taking out his wallet)*

Check in with me tomorrow, we'll see where we are.

(Kai tries to put money on the table. Jack stops him.)

JACK: One more round?

KAI: I'm afraid not.

JACK: The wife to get home to.

KAI: That's right.

JACK: I say that with admiration.

KAI: Thanks for the drink, Jack. And the chair. Have I properly thanked you for the chair yet? We like our chair.

JACK: I'm glad you like it. Do you really? Because understanding what goes into a chairÉthat's a huge enterprise, if you can believe. People have spent years, years of their lives on a single chair. Maybe that sounds silly to you, but I think it's quite moving, to think about the body, to think about gravity and structure and stability and rest -- I'm really just at the beginning of understanding what makes a good chair.

KAI: I think you've done very well.

(Kai pats Jack's back, starts to go.)

JACK: There's this amazing chair … this guy Pesce, totally brilliant, he did this chair … late sixties, '68 I think … it's a round, red … obscenely red, soft, pliable, wide, bad-ass chair. He modeled it on the Venus of Wilhendorf.

KAI: What's that?

JACK: I'm sure you've seen the image somewhere … classic fertility goddess. And you're meant to sink into this chair, this chair that's abstracted from the shape of a woman in an exaggerated cartoon way, and the footstool's this big red sphere tied to the leg like a ball and chain. Pesce says he saw a woman as a prisoner of herself against her will, and he wanted to convey that.

(Kai nods, standing, his coat in hand. Jack is lost for a moment, facing out.)

But I've sat in that chair, I've been engulfed by the Venus, and I felt quite sure that it was the other way around, that the prisoner was me.

KAI: A prisoner of the woman, or a prisoner of you own nature?

JACK: I'll have to think about that. I will think about that.

(Kai goes, leaving Jack alone at the bar.)

Extinction
Gabe McKinley

Seriocomic
Max, 30's
Finn, 30's

Max and Finn, best friends since collage, take an annual pleasure seeking vacation, during which they ply themselves with booze, drugs and women, but this year things have changed.

MAX: I just thought of that girl Ashley. The one we shared in Vegas.

FINN: You told her I was a podiatrist. I spent half the night examining her arches.

MAX: Jesus, it was like sticking my dick in a beehive.

FINN: Desperate times call for desperate measures.

MAX: Desperate is right... She was something else. If you add it up. How many times?

FINN: How many times?

MAX: Have I gotten you laid?

FINN: You? Fuck you. I can do... I have done okay on my own, thank you very much. Pulled my weight. You're getting senile in your old age.

MAX: A real swinging dick, huh? Let's settle this once and for all. Come on. Let's see it. Winner buys dinner.

FINN: What are you...?

MAX: Wait. Length or girth? Both?

FINN: Are you serious?

MAX: Come on. I'll call the front desk and get a ruler. Not enough room? Yard stick? Should I open the door?

FINN: Fuck you. I'm not...

MAX: The look on your face. I'll buy dinner anyway.

FINN: No. Just put some fucking pants on.

MAX: I insist. What time is it?

FINN: *(checking)*

Five minutes since the last time you asked.

MAX: Close enough. Time to stop, drop and roll...

Max finds his drugs and starts to cut up some lines. He rolls up a dollar bill.

FINN: Really?

MAX: I seem to remember last time you were a hoover. There was never enough. Like a fucking anteater.

Max snorts a line.

MAX: *(cont'd)*

Sweet Jesus, I'm home. The shampoo effect.

FINN: *(remembering)*

Wash, rinse, repeat.

Max snorts another line. He offers Finn the bill.

MAX: Your turn.

FINN: No thank you. Look, Max there's...

MAX: Why don't you go shower?

FINN: Listen man...

MAX: You can borrow a shirt. Because you aren't getting laid looking like that unless we happen upon a meeting of young homosexual communists. Maybe not even then.

FINN: Are you listening?

MAX: Yes, Finn. Yes. I'm listening.

FINN: I'm going to have a baby.

Silence.

MAX: Odd. You're not even showing. With a girl?

FINN: Yeah, with a girl.

MAX: Your first time?

FINN: What do you mean?

MAX: You must've? At some point before... All the...? It's not the first time you've gotten a girl pregnant, is it?

FINN: Yes.

MAX: Oh boy, you're in it now, boy... It happened to me once. It happens to the best of us.

FINN: When?

MAX: Before. Does it matter?

FINN: This is different?

MAX: I don't think it is.

FINN: This isn't a one night stand.

MAX: Oh, you two are together?

FINN: We're having a baby.

MAX: We're having a baby? Me and you? Are you going to make an honest man out of me?

FINN: I don't know, is it possible?

MAX: So...?

FINN: So...she's due in the fall.

MAX: Wow. I guess we both came baring news, huh?

FINN: *(a look)*

MAX: Well. Congratulations are in order, I guess.   Congratulations. Tell me... who's the proud mama?

FINN: Her name is Susan. Susan Poland.

MAX: Wait, Susan Poland? Not NYU Susan?

FINN: The same.

MAX: Holy shit, the actress? I remember her. I remember her.

FINN: Oh yeah?

MAX: Yeah. I think I fucked her. *(Beat)* I'm just kidding.

FINN: You prick. We reconnected a while ago and... started talking... It's funny actually...

MAX: Is it?

FINN: Is it what?

MAX: Is it funny?

FINN: I mean in the ironic...

MAX: ...You always had a thing for her. Good for you. Really? An actress?

FINN: Former.

MAX: A former writer and a former actress... Jesus the Boulevard of Broken Dreams. Remember that girl, Julie? She was an actress and she was a real bunny boiler. She hid in my closet.

FINN: That Julie girl wasn't an actress, she did burlesque.

MAX: What's wrong with burlesque? It's the best thing to happen to fat chicks since black guys.

FINN: *(ignoring the last remark)*

Susan is back at school. That's where we met again. She's studying Social Policy.

MAX: Oh my God... good for her. For you. This calls for a celebration, or at least a drowning of sorrows. Let's talk about it over some cocktails.

FINN: Yeah. Drinks are fine, talking is fine... but I don't want to...ah...

Max stands, going toward the door.

MAX: It's a wonder you quit writing you're so fucking articulate.

FINN: I don't want to spend the whole night chasing women.

MAX: What are you talking about?

FINN: Not like before. I can't. With the baby and all... Just so we're on the same page.

MAX: The hits just keep on coming with you... You're killing me here. It's just us.

FINN: Max. Look. I know. But everything has changed.

MAX: It doesn't have to. Your secret is safe with me, Finn. Let's go. This is our weekend, right? Everything is confidentiAL:

FINN: I don't want to lie to her.

Gizmo Love
John Kolvenbach

Seriocomic
Max, late 30s
Thomas, early 30s

> *Max and Thomas are career criminals. Max is somewhat older, he's the boss. Thomas looks up to Max, considers him a mentor. Before this scene takes place, Max and Thomas attempted to rob a man who Thomas shot impulsively. Max considers this a breech of protocol.*

MAX: How many times are we going to go *through* this? Thomas [At least one more, it looks like.]

MAX: You have a Passive Subject, Thomas, He had *soiled* himself for Goddsake.

THOMAS: I know, that was disgusting.

MAX: Did you *look* at this guy? Before you decide to *shoot* him for no reason?

THOMAS: I didn't *decide* anything.-

MAX: He was a *Nanny.*

THOMAS: I didn't *decide* Max, It was instinct. Max It was *what?*

THOMAS: I had an instinct.

MAX: *(Beat.)* [You know, you'd think, over a *lifetime,* you like to believe that at least *some* of what you offer might actually be *received-*

THOMAS: Can we change the subject here, Max?

MAX: He was *Compliant.*

THOMAS: I don't think so.

MAX: He shit his *pants,* Thomas, this *Enthusiast,* What do you *want?* Thomas He Moved.

(Beat.)

MAX: Do you forget that I was *Standing* there? That I was Standing Right There?

THOMAS: I saw him move.

MAX: He Did *Not* [and even if he *had,* so a man, picked last his whole *life,* this guy scratches his *elbow* -

THOMAS: I'm not saying he scratched his elbow.

MAX: He was *Compliant!* On my *request,* this man Unlocked his own *Door.* I had only to *Ask!*

THOMAS: "Get outta the cah."

(Beat.)

MAX: Excuse me?

THOMAS: That's how you said it. "Get outta de cah." Max What in Sam Hill are you talking about.

THOMAS: I was Standing there.

MAX: That is *not* how I say that.

THOMAS: "get outta de cah."

MAX: Are you *joking?* An Accent? Why would I do that? Thomas I don't know.

MAX: In a *Professional Situation,* I'm a Vaudevillian? What are you saying? I'm an *Impressionist?*

THOMAS: Sometimes when we're on a job

MAX: What *is* this? *"sometimes"?* You've got a fucking Theory here Thomas? You've got *Examples?*

THOMAS: I've *noticed* something.

MAX: You're a spy. You watch me *Sleep,* You take my *Pulse* when I'm *Napping,* you have a *Chart.*

THOMAS: Now don't get all crazy.

MAX: Who you *Shot* this guy, by the way, while we're slinging arrows, I may have *mispronounced,* which I *didn't,* I made a *request,* in *Accepted Parlance*- [You think I'm a *Cartoon?* What do I *gain?* In front of a *subject,* Thomas?] Why Would I Do that?

THOMAS: you want them to love you.

(Pause.)

THOMAS: It's what I think, Max.

(Pause.)

MAX: Thomas, Christ.

THOMAS: It might be one of those unconscious things.

MAX: good lord.

THOMAS: You might not be *aware* of it.

MAX: Thomas.

THOMAS: It's only *natural,* a guy wants to be appreciated.

MAX: I have *you.*

(Pause.)

THOMAS: [You *have* me, you said?]

MAX: I need love? It's what you're saying: Max tries to please, Max needs love from strangers.

THOMAS: Ok.

MAX: and I'm saying well how about this: I have you. *(Pause.)*

THOMAS: Oh.

MAX: Right?

THOMAS: Max Thank you very much.

MAX: You're welcome.
  (Pause.)
THOMAS: I have you too.
MAX: Yes you do.

Jailbait
Deirdre O'Connor

Seriocomic
Robert, early 30s
Mark, early 30s

Robert, a newly single thirty-something, attempts to ease the pain of his divorce by going to a club on a date set up by his friend Mark; but when Robert gets to the club and discovers nothing but throbbing music and twenty-year olds he begins to have second thoughts about Mark's plan.

A large, modern, impersonal club.

Robert, an analyst with a loosened tie leans against the wall in a secluded corner. He is in his mid 30s but looks older. Muted music thumps through the wall behind him. Robert has a cell phone in his hand. He opens it, contemplates dialing, then closes it again. Robert paces. He pulls off his tie, rolls it up, and sticks it in his back pocket. He opens the phone again and dials.

ROBERT: So... Hey. It's me. I know we said we wouldn't call and I'm sorry but... I'm calling. Obviously. I wasn't going to but it's just- I got this package today. From your Mom, actually. And it had been mislabeled so... It must've been kicking around the mail room for... A while. And I uh... I almost didn't open it because... I just felt like I didn't have the right to something that was intended for... For probably us. But us of a different time. Yeah. But I opened it and it was, uh... It was Goodnight, Moon. And she wrote this really lovely little note on the first page. Obviously, obviously before.... Everything. And I don't... I don't know what to do with it, you know? And I thought maybe you would want it, but... Why would you want it? Just... I can't throw it out. And I thought. I don't know what I thought. I just called. Because...I want to talk. If you do. And if you don't, well you can let me know by not calling.   Extending this already excruciating silence. But if you do, then just call. And we can... I have no idea. We can something. Just call.
(Robert closes his phone.)
Shit.
(MARK, also in his mid 30s, enters with a drink in his hand. Mark is dressed in his going out clothes. Designer jeans and a black fitted sweater. He looks

years younger than Robert and is obviously more at home in the club. Mark leans against the wall next to Robert. Robert slips his cell phone back into his pocket.)

MARK: Nice slacks.

ROBERT: What?

MARK: Slacks.

ROBERT: Oh.

MARK: You wear those to work?

ROBERT: Yeah.

MARK: And then you wore them here.

ROBERT: So?

MARK: So they're work pants.

ROBERT: They're pants. Pants are pants.

MARK: Pants are not pants.

ROBERT: I'm sorry?

MARK: Did you even go home and change?

ROBERT: I took off my tie.

MARK: You took off your--
     (Mark sees the edge of Robert's tie sticking out of his back pocket. He grabs it and pulls it out.)
     You didn't even go home.

ROBERT: I had a lot of work.

MARK: Work.

ROBERT: Baker's giving me automotives. Do you know how hard it is to follow automotives?

MARK: You mean cars?

ROBERT: Yeah.

MARK: So just say cars.

ROBERT: It's a lot of work.

MARK: Fine. Fine.

ROBERT: So I came right from work.

MARK: It's just... I thought you were serious, but...

ROBERT: Come on.

MARK: You came right from work. You didn't change. You didn't shave.

ROBERT: I shaved this morning.

MARK: Well, you look like ass.

ROBERT: Thanks.

MARK: Hey, you asked for my help here.

ROBERT: I asked for a distraction.

MARK: A female distraction. You know this will involve some effort on your part.

ROBERT: This is how I dress. This is how I've always dressed.

MARK: This is how relationship Robert dressed. This is the off-the-market look. It's the look that says, "I'm just here for one drink because I've got a lady waiting at home and we've removed into our comfortable stage." Do you have a lady waiting at home?

ROBERT: Jesus, Mark.

MARK: Hey, I'm just trying to help here.

ROBERT: By pouring salt in my wounds?

MARK: What salt? What salt? It's a little thing called: honesty.

ROBERT: Fine. I get it.

MARK: I can only do so much, you know?

ROBERT: I get it.

MARK: I can only bring the chick to water. But you gotta put away the Brooks Brothers if you want her to drink.

ROBERT: I don't even know what that means.

MARK: It means you've failed me.

ROBERT: I'm sorry.

MARK: I got you a girl, and you failed me.

ROBERT: And where is this girl?

MARK: She's coming.

ROBERT: But she's not here.

MARK: She's coming.

ROBERT: My point is you can't go demanding praise for a job well done when the job's not... Well, done.

MARK: They'll be here.

ROBERT: Here.

MARK: Here in this club. Not here in this exact spot. We'll have to keep circulating.

ROBERT: Jesus.

MARK: Don't be such a lazy fuck.

ROBERT: This just isn't what I pictured.

MARK: What did you picture?

ROBERT: I don't know. A restaurant, maybe. Or a wine bar.
    (Mark scoffs.)
    Or a regular bar. Just a regular bar would've been fine.

MARK: There's a regular bar here.

ROBERT: But it's a club.

MARK: So?

ROBERT: So, have you noticed that every other person here is, I don't know...
22?

MARK: No, they're dressed like they're 22. Do you see the subtle difference?

ROBERT: Just don't make me "circulate." When I circulate I feel like a
voyeuristic, dirty old man.

MARK: Would you stop saying old? If you're old, I'm old. And I refuse to be old.
Besides, what we now lack in hairline, we make up for in bank account.

ROBERT: At least tell me she's funny.

MARK: She's funny.

ROBERT: And smart enough to carry on a somewhat interesting conversation?

MARK: She goes to Harvard.

ROBERT: That means nothing. Lots of stupid girls go to Harvard.

MARK: This girl's a freaking genius. Summa cum whatever.

ROBERT:OK.

(Pause.)

You have met this girl, right?

MARK: Would you give me some credit?

ROBERT: That wasn't a yes.

MARK: I've met her, I've met her.

ROBERT: And what did you tell her about me?

MARK: You know, stuff.

ROBERT: But did you get into specifics?

MARK: Nothing specific, no.

ROBERT: Did you tell her I'm just coming off a serious--

MARK: Do you think I want to depress her with that shit? Jesus. No, I didn't
tell her about your breakup.

ROBERT: You didn't tell her any lies did you? If you lied to her I need to know.

MARK: I didn't lie to her.

ROBERT: So what'd you say?

MARK: I said, uhm... That you were my friend and...

ROBERT: You've never laid eyes on her.

MARK: OK, I've never technically laid eyes on her.

ROBERT: Fuck.

MARK: What? I don't have time to audition every prospective piece of ass.

ROBERT: This was a bad idea.

MARK: Could you stop being such a whiny bitch for a minute? You wanted to go out, so we're out. You wanted to meet someone so I got you a beautiful girl to keep you company. What is your problem?

ROBERT: You don't actually know if she's beautiful.

MARK: She's beautiful.

ROBERT: How do you know that?

MARK: Look, if she's ugly, I'll fuck her. OK?

ROBERT: That's comforting. Thanks.

MARK: Hey, it's all about getting you a good time.

(Robert pulls his cell phone out of his pocket and checks it.)

Stop checking that thing.

ROBERT: What? I was checking the time.

MARK: She hasn't called.

ROBERT: She who? I was checking the time.

MARK: Really? What time is it?

ROBERT: It's... Uh....

(Robert clearly doesn't know. He tries to discreetly peer at his cell phone again.)

Ten-thirty. It's ten-thirty.

MARK: I'm gonna snap that thing in half.

ROBERT: I'm sorry. I felt vibrating. I thought it was vibrating. I think it was just the floor.

MARK: She's not going to call. And she better not call because if she calls then I'm going to answer and tell her to stop calling and fucking with your head.

ROBERT: We have unresolved issues.

MARK: You have unresolved issues. She just likes to check in to make sure you're still miserable before she kicks you in the teeth again.

ROBERT: OK, just because you don't like her--

MARK: I don't like this. If you called me up last month and told me you were getting married? Fine. You were practically dead to me anyway. But you told me you broke up.

ROBERT: We did.

MARK: So act like it.

ROBERT: I can't just turn it off, you know?

MARK: No. I don't know. I don't know how you turned it on in the first place.

ROBERT: Yeah, you talk a big game.

MARK: I play a big game.

ROBERT: It's gonna be you again, someday.

MARK: No. Never again.

ROBERT: That's what you say, but then you're gonna meet some girl and all of a sudden you're gonna be putting down cash for some little house in Belmont and daydreaming about fucking Lamaze classes.

MARK: Bullshit. My first wife hasn't even been born yet.

ROBERT: That's what you say.

(Mark looks at Robert a moment.)

MARK: *(carefully)* You didn't... want all that. Did you?

ROBERT: What?

MARK: With Valerie. All that shit about the house and the baby and the--

ROBERT: I was just talking.

MARK: Oh.

(Pause.)

ROBERT: Besides. What's that compared to all this?

(Robert takes a long drink from his beer and scans the room.)

The Long Red Road
Brett C. Leonard

Dramatic
Sammy, 35
Bob, 36

> *Sammy and Bob haven't seen each other in nine years, ever since Sammy ran off after a tragic drunk-driving accident which resulted in the death of one daughter and the maiming of his wife. His other daughter, Tasha, survived. She has been living with Bob for the past nine years, along with her mother, who lost her legs in the accident. Bob and Tasha have just driven from Kansas to see Sammy. Tasha has run off, and Sammy's new girlfriend, Annie, has gone to look for her. Sammy and Bob here confront each other for the first time since the accident.*

BOB: They went lookin' for you.
   (Pause.)
SAMMY: Ya want a drink?
BOB: I'm alright.
   (Beat.)
SAMMY: No?
   (Beat.)
BOB: No.
   (Pause.)
SAMMY: Cuz ya gotta drive?
BOB: I quit.
   (Pause.)
   (Sammy goes to the kitchen. He stands on a chair and takes a hidden bottle out of a ceramic vase on top of the cabinet. He gets down from the chair and pours himself a drink. He moves to the table and looks at Tasha's drawings.)
SAMMY: Pretty good. Not bad.
   He continues to look at Tasha's drawings. He lights a cigarette. He offers one to BOB.
SAMMY: Smoke?
BOB: No.
SAMMY: Ya quit that too?
BOB: Got my own.
   (Sammy continues looking at the drawings.) (Pause.)

SAMMY: How old she now? She eleven or twelve?

BOB: Thirteen.

SAMMY: Mmmm.

BOB: Almost fourteen.

SAMMY: Mmmm.

   (Bob lights a cigarette.)

SAMMY: Really, these, uh...these drawin's...mmm...*(beat)* Sandy come too?

BOB: [No].

SAMMY: Huh?

BOB: No.

SAMMY: *(Pause.)*

   You look alright. Better'n I'd a 'spected, I suppose.

BOB: I wanna leave Tasha here with you.

SAMMY: Whaddaya mean?

BOB: Yeah.

SAMMY: What's that mean, wanna leave her?

BOB: I'm gonna leave her with you an' head back without her. Unless you wanna come with, then we can go all three.

SAMMY: I don't think so, no.

BOB: Which one?

SAMMY: Mmmph?

BOB: Which one you say "no" about? Leavin' her here or you comin' with?

SAMMY: I don't like neither one.

BOB: I can't be around them no more, Sam. I gave nine-odd years.

SAMMY: You're her Godfather, that's the oath you took.

BOB: In case anything happened to you.

SAMMY: Some'n did happen. Your job's ta take care an' see they alright - it don't have no nine-year expiration, that's for life.

BOB: It's been for life already.

SAMMY: No, it's been nine years.

BOB: My whole life's livin' 'bout you.

SAMMY: You took a oath, Bob, you know better.

BOB: Not so you could up an' run off, I didn't.

SAMMY: In case anything happened to my girls an' some'n happened! It's a promise for life ta take care, fuck you.

BOB: I need ta leave her here or I need you ta return. Are ya gonna return?

SAMMY: There's no time-limit on what occurred - I go back I'm put in state pen. Why in goddamn hell I'm a do some'n like that?

BOB: It was good ta see ya. Tell yer lady friend I said thanks

   (Bob moves toward the door.)

SAMMY: Where you goin'? Hey - where the fuck you goin'?! I CAN'T HAVE HER HERE WITH ME! BOBBY?! I can't.

BOB: But she's yours.

SAMMY: I can't take care a' myself.

BOB: You gotchyer pretty lil girlfriend ta help.

SAMMY: This ain't no good here, Bobby. It ain't good.

    (Beat.)

    You always been more on your own feet, ya know? I never seemed ta find me no solid ground, quicksand. It's better with you. It's better.

BOB: *(Beat.)*

    Did Daddy ever take you out to the barn?

SAMMY: Whaddaya mean?

BOB: Did he ever take you out there with him?

SAMMY: I dunno.

BOB: No?

SAMMY: Not that I remember, I dunno.

BOB: For some father-son time? Just the two a' you?

SAMMY: No.

BOB: Sure?

SAMMY: Maybe ta feed somethin' or whatever, why?

BOB: *(Beat.)*

    Where do they keep their retarded here, Sammy? Here, in Indian Land?

SAMMY: I dunno.

BOB: How bout Kansas? Where do we keep the retarded there?

SAMMY: In the basement.

BOB: An' do we let'm come out an' play from time ta time?

SAMMY: No.

BOB: Or come up in the house on Thanksgiving?

SAMMY: I said no.

BOB: How 'bout Christmas? Or Easter? We ever let'm come up an' eat, 'steada bringin' 'em food down in the dark?

SAMMY: No.

BOB: Never?

SAMMY: No.

BOB: *(Beat.)*

    I better go, it's twelve hours. I don't wanna haveta pull over take a room.

SAMMY: You can't leave!

BOB: I get thoughts, Sam.

SAMMY: Whaddaya mean?

BOB: I get thoughts.

SAMMY: Everybody gets thoughts, so what, thoughts? C'mon buddy, have a drink with me, what's a lil' one gonna do ya?

BOB: I told you I quit.

SAMMY: Nobody goddamn drinks no more.

BOB: About Tasha.

SAMMY: What about her?

BOB: I gotta go.

SAMMY: You ain't got her in the basement, do ya?

BOB: No.

SAMMY: Somethin' with the accident got her messed in the head?

BOB: She's in your old room, Sam - the one with the lock on the door.

SAMMY: She ain't messed none from the accident?

BOB: No.

SAMMY: What about Sandra, she alright?

BOB: She's fine.

SAMMY: What about her legs?

BOB: They're beautiful.

SAMMY: Yeah?

BOB: Yeah.

SAMMY: Cuz they ain't look beautiful that night.

BOB: I live with them, Sam.

SAMMY: Who?

BOB: Sandra and Tasha.

SAMMY: That's good, yeah.

BOB: I've lived with 'em all nine years since that night.

SAMMY: Well, ya suppose to - ya took a oath.

BOB: Maybe a lil' different arrangement than you might 'speck. Sandra was in the hospital, Lindy was dead...mom an' pop gone. Someone hadda be there for Tasha. An' when Sandy got back, well... I just sorta stayed on.

SAMMY: Ya already said that.

BOB: You got everything an' got away with everything our whole life. You get three nights in a cornfield, I get three nights in the barn.

SAMMY: What're ya talkin' 'bout, cornfield?

BOB: I share a bed with your wife, Sam. In your bed, in your house...the house mom an' pop left YOU in the will, my younger brother got the goddamn house.

SAMMY: I was married with two kids. You still ain't over this bullshit? Hell, you been in nine years, you had more'n twice as long.

BOB: I fuck your wife, Sam! Every night I have relations with your horny beautiful wife! I fuck her, Sam. I fuck'r good, I fuck'r hard, and I fuck'r in your bed!

SAMMY: So?

BOB: So?

SAMMY: So what?

The Man Who Ate Michael Rockefeller

Jeff Cohen

Seriocomic
Designing Man, 20s
Half-Moon Terror, 20s

> *In* **The Man Who Ate Michael Rockefeller**, *a master wood carver tells the story of Michael Rockefeller's encounters with the primitive Asmat people of New Guinea. In 1961 the 23 year-old Rockefeller, the son of New York Governor Nelson Rockefeller, disappeared in this remote region and was never heard from again. The mystery of his disappearance remains unsolved to this day. In this scene, the master carver Designing Man and his warrior best friend Half-Moon Terror discuss the political ramifications surrounding the sudden death of their village chief soon after Rockefeller's visit.*

DESIGNING MAN: *(to Audience)*
Two days after his boat pulled away, our Governor was found dead in his hut.
(Half-Moon walks up to Designing Man.)
HALF-MOON: Well?
DESIGNING MAN: Well what?
HALF-MOON: What do you think?
DESIGNING MAN: About what?
HALF-MOON: Don't be dense. There wasn't even a wound. It's as though he fell down and his spirit simply leapt out of him. And you don't have an opinion about it?
DESIGNING MAN: What kind of opinion should I have?
HALF-MOON: Not for me to say. But the underchiefs are furious as I'm sure you know.
DESIGNING MAN: As well they should be.
HALF-MOON: They speculate and they speculate and they speculate. You know how they do.
DESIGNING MAN: Yes.
HALF-MOON: How it's all on account of Rockefeller. How the Governor and the billionaire's doctor had spent time conversing. That the billionaire's doctor poisoned him. Or hexed him. Lots of speculation.
DESIGNING MAN: No doubt.
HALF-MOON: And now things are out of balance. Between our tribe and

Rockefeller's.

DESIGNING MAN: So what are you getting at?

HALF-MOON: Me? I'm getting at nothing. I'm not the one spec-ulating.

DESIGNING MAN: Uh huh.

HALF-MOON: You know what would have happened in the old days.

DESIGNING MAN: What would've happened.

HALF-MOON: Before we became polluted with certain – virtues. Imported virtues. You know, right?

DESIGNING MAN: Half-Moon Terror. If you have something you want to tell me than I wish you'd stop beating around the bush and just tell me.

HALF-MOON: All I'm saying is that an imbalance such as this one – someone of equal power in the rival tribe would have to part with their head.

(A pause for emphasis.)

This means Rockefeller.

DESIGNING MAN: I see.

HALF-MOON: But, then, you're the one who's got the deal going with him.

DESIGNING MAN: So? Is that supposed to mean something? I'm supposed to say either way? That's what you're getting at?

HALF-MOON: Listen closely, Designing Man. Our Governor is dead. We're leaderless. Until a new one's appointed the entire Council's got to agree on how to handle this. And you, Master Carver, are a key player in the Council.

DESIGNING MAN: You sound like fucking Bringing Man right now, you know that?

HALF-MOON: I'm just saying.

DESIGNING MAN: Look. However the Governor died, that man, Rockefeller, is no enemy. You can't prove it's Rockefeller's fault:…

HALF-MOON: I didn't say it was his fault…

DESIGNING MAN: Are you playing word games with me now? Are you trying to be like Bringing Man? Half-Moon, next to my own wife, Rockefeller just might be the least injurious soul I've ever met.

HALF-MOON: *(laughing slightly)*

Why? Because he's a fan of your work? Because he likes to eat?

DESIGNING MAN: Look. You have a point. I don't know what it is about Rockefeller. But I feel like I want to protect him. There's an earnestness about him, a naïve thirst to be brothers – it's very unusual for a white man.

HALF-MOON: I will agree that he is unusuAL:

DESIGNING MAN: When I try to imagine taking his head I can only see stars pouring out of his neck and a flock of enraged spirits descending on us, screaming.

HALF-MOON: So what are you saying?

DESIGNING MAN: If it comes to a vote in the Council?

HALF-MOON: Yes.

DESIGNING MAN: Then I'm voting "no."

HALF-MOON: You're sure?

DESIGNING MAN: Yes.

HALF-MOON: Then I have to tell you that there are council-members who have an argument with that decision. I saw them and they were speaking harshly and gesturing at your hut. And I did what I could to calm them down.

DESIGNING MAN: I appreciate that.

HALF-MOON: Not a problem. Anyway, I just wanted to give you a head's up. So to speak.

DESIGNING MAN: Yes. So to speak.

(Half-Moon leaves. Designing Man watches him go.)

Office Hours

A. R. Gurney

Seriocomic
Richard, late 20s
Jerry, early 20s

> *Richard, a college professor, teaches a section of required course on the Great Books. Jerry, one of his students, has come to his office to ask him a personal question.*

> *(Richard, an instructor, comes on, carrying his books and Notes. Jerry, a student, appears in the doorway)*

RICHARD: *(noticing him)*
    Hi there.

JERRY: Isn't this your office hours?

RICHARD: It is indeed.

JERRY: I thought it was.

RICHARD: Come on in.
    (Jerry steps into the office)
    Um. Let me think. Jerry, Right?

JERRY: Right. May I shut the door?

RICHARD: You want the door shut?

JERRY: This is kind of personAL:

RICHARD: Shut the door then. By all means.
    (Jerry does)
And please sit down.
    (Jerry does. A pause)

JERRY: Um. May I ask a personal question?

RICHARD: Ask away.

JERRY: Are you …?

RICHARD: Am I what?

JERRY: Are you gay, Professor?
    (a moment)

RICHARD: Call me Richard, if you want. The administration thinks it helps
    break the ice.

JERRY: I might feel weird doing that.

RICHARD: Give it a try.

JERRY: O.K., Richard.

RICHARD: Good.

JERRY: So. Are you gay, Richard?

(Pause.)

RICHARD: Yes.

JERRY: You are?

RICHARD: Yes.

JERRY: Thought so.

RICHARD: What made you think so?

JERRY: When we were doing Plato, you sort of said so.

RICHARD: I did, didn't I? When we took that side excursion into Plato's Symposium, I may have outed myself.

JERRY: Did you want to out yourself?

RICHARD: I did and didn't.

JERRY: Was Plato gay?

RICHARD: Scholars think he may have been.

JERRY: Saint Paul was gay.

RICHARD: Says who?

JERRY: My roommate's instructor. Paul talks in one of his letters about the thorn in his side. He thinks being gay is a thorn.

RICHARD: I suppose it can be.

JERRY: I think it is. Because I'm gay, too.

RICHARD: Oh really?

JERRY: Could you tell?

RICHARD: I don't know you well enough to think either way.

JERRY: They're starting up a Gay Alliance here, did you know that? For Gay Students and Faculty.

RICHARD: I knew that. Yes.

JERRY: Have you gone to any meetings?

RICHARD: No.

JERRY: You could go, you know. They're very welcoming.

RICHARD: I'm sure they are.

JERRY: I've gone. Several times. Why won't you go?

RICHARD: It may be too reductive a way of defining one's self..

JERRY: Saying you're gay?

RICHARD: We are other things as well.

JERRY: I go there to meet people.

RICHARD: Sounds like as good a place as any.

JERRY: It's a better place than most. Because you have things in common .

RICHARD: What can I do for you, Jerry?

JERRY: I keep thinking of The Confessions of Saint Augustine …

RICHARD: Do you like the book?

JERRY: No I don't, actually.

RICHARD: I'm sorry.

JERRY: Too much Catholic bullshit. Too much "Forgive me, Father, for I have sinned."

RICHARD: There's a lot of that.

JERRY: Except I keep thinking about the part where Saint Augustine talks about his buddy Alipus?

RICHARD: A- lip-i- us.

JERRY: Alipius. Remember when he talks about Alipius getting hooked on the gladiatorial games at the local coliseum.

RICHARD: Oh yes.

JERRY: Alypius knows the games are bad, with all that blood and gore right in front of you, and sometimes guys actually killing each other! But he can't stay away.

RICHARD: Exactly.

JERRY: In fact, one time he goes just to test himself. And he covers his eyes, and swears he's not going to look, but the cheering of the crowd hooks him, and pretty soon he's looking and cheering with the best of them, watching guys slaughter each other.

RICHARD: That's it.

JERRY: So he realizes he's hooked. He's an addict. Until Saint Augustine points him toward God. And that helps Alipius give up the games.

RICHARD: You've read the Confessions very thoroughly.

JERRY: Just that part. Because I identified with Alypius.

RICHARD: You're addicted to games?

JERRY: I'm addicted to sex.

(Pause.)

Gay sex.

RICHARD: Addicted?

JERRY: I think about it all the time. Sometimes I go to the gay alliance not to fight for our rights, but just to meet other guys. And it's not just there. Everywhere I go, I check guys out. Is he gay? What's he like with his clothes off? What's he like in bed?

RICHARD: At least you keep it in bed.

JERRY: You mean, rather than in some back alley? Don't be so sure. I'm a real whore, Richard..

RICHARD: Easy now.

JERRY: I am. Except I don't get paid.

RICHARD: You're saying you're promiscuous.

JERRY: That's putting it mildly

RICHARD: I don't think promiscuity is a good idea, Jerry.

JERRY: I know it isn't.

RICHARD: So what are you saying?

JERRY: I want to kick the habit. Like Alypius did..

RICHARD: AS Alipius did.

JERRY: As Alipius did. The problem is, he had Saint Augustine's help. Which means God's help. Most addicts need some higher power to kick the habit. I know that because my Dad was an alkie. Now he goes to church and that helps him.

RICHARD: Glad to hear it.

JERRY: Though my Dad says God will have me burn in hell unless I stop being gay..

RICHARD: Ah yes.

JERRY: But I can't turn to God, because I don't believe that stuff.

RICHARD: So?

JERRY: So I'm turning to you. Richard.

RICHARD: Me?

JERRY: You've worked it out, haven't you, Richard. You're cool in class, and easy outside.

RICHARD: I try to be.

JERRY: Oh come on. I've checked you out. I know you live with another guy.

RICHARD: Yes I do.

JERRY: He sings in an a capella group down at the Y.

RICHARD: You've done your homework, haven't you?

JERRY: Sure have. I went and saw him there. He looks like a nice guy. The program said he was a lawyer.

RICHARD: He is. He's a good one.

JERRY: I hear you even take him to parties.

RICHARD: Some parties.

JERRY: Faculty parties.

RICHARD: Some faculty parties.

JERRY: That takes guts, it seems to me. I saw you together at one of the basket ball games. You seemed easy with it.

RICHARD: Not so easy.

JERRY: Easier than I'd be.

RICHARD: You've been doing a lot of research.

JERRY: That's because I want you to take me on.

RICHARD: Take you on?

JERRY: As a mentor. Like those sponsors you get in AA. Or like Saint Augustine did for Alypius. So I could call you when I'm … when I'm tempted to visit the gladiatorial games..

RICHARD: I'm no saint, Jerry.

JERRY: Hey. Like Saint Augustine says, the greatest sinners make the greatest saints.

RICHARD: I don't see it as a sin.

JERRY: Hey that's it. It's not a bad thing, for you. It's not like the games in the Coliseum.

RICHARD: I should hope not.

JERRY: You've got it together. I admire that. I got for that.

RICHARD: Thank you.

JERRY: So couldn't we do stuff together? Occasionally? For example, do you like to hike? Maybe we could hike together some time. Your friend, too, of course, if he'd like to come.. Or do you run? I've taken up running lately. To tamp down the hormones. Know what I mean?

RICHARD: I do.

JERRY: I could use someone to run with, Richard.

(Pause.)

Richard? Did you hear me?

RICHARD: I did.

JERRY: So will you be my buddy?

RICHARD: Like the buddy system in some summer camp?

JERRY: What's wrong with that? That's so kids won't drown. Because sometimes I think I'm drowning, Richard.

RICHARD: Oh now…

JERRY: How about it?

RICHARD: I'm not sure, Jerry.

JERRY: Not sure about me?

RICHARD: Not sure about myself. If I were straight, and you were a female, I'd probably say yes, and we'd slide into the sack within a month. This place is riddled with faculty-student relationships like that. It happens a lot. The divorces happen later.

JERRY: You think stuff could happen between you and me?

RICHARD: It might.

JERRY: Would that be a bad thing?

RICHARD: Yes.

JERRY: It wouldn't be for me.

RICHARD: It would be for me.

JERRY: You could lose your job, I guess.

RICHARD: I'd lose much more than that.

(Pause.)

JERRY: Do you know the Rainbow Grille over on Front Street?

RICHARD: Heard of it. Yes.

JERRY: I sometimes hang out there.

RICHARD: Oh yes?

JERRY: Could we at least meet there sometime and talk?

RICHARD: I don't think so.

JERRY: Just to talk?

RICHARD: I really don't think so.

JERRY: You could bring along your friend.

RICHARD: No.

JERRY: Not a good idea, right?

RICHARD: Right.

JERRY: *(getting up)*

I'll be there this coming Saturday evening.

RICHARD: I won't be.

JERRY: If you don't show up, I'll understand.

(He stops at the door)

Shall I leave the door open?

RICHARD: If you would.

(Jerry goes. Richard remains at his desk, staring out. Then he opens his book, tries to work.)

Radio Free Emerson
Paul Grellong

Seriocomic.
Henry and Al, 30s.

> *Henry and Al were friends when they were younger. They haven't seen each other in many years. Henry is a struggling contractor and would-be architect. Al works lobster boats in Maine. Today they meet again at the funeral service for Al's father. A few hours after the reception, Al shows up at Henry's apartment unannounced. Henry's wife Gina, drunk on white wine, just exited so the two men could be alone to catch up. Henry is embarrassed about the size of his apartment. He's also embarrassed about something else, something very personal he confesses to* AL: *In the past few years Al has developed a strange philosophy. Now he's determined to make his old friend see the light.*

HENRY: Wine.

AL: Yeah.

HENRY: And women!

AL: When they're thin ...

HENRY: Forget about it, they don't stand a chance. Men, though -

AL: It's a different thing.

HENRY: Entirely different. *(They toast by clinking bottlenecks.)* Really wish we had known you were coming. Gina could have cleaned.

AL: Doesn't matter.

HENRY: Place is a mess.

AL: Hey ...

HENRY: Oh - can I show you the house? Let me get the model.

AL: The doctor's house?

HENRY: Ours. *(From a table in the corner of the room, Henry picks up a model. He carries it to the coffee table and places it down in front of Al, Removes a cover.)* What do you think?

AL: It's beautiful. You designed this?

HENRY: Yes. I've been planning a house like this since grad school. The doctor's I'm building from plans he downloaded off the Internet.

AL: Really?

HENRY: People are doing that now. *(Pause.)* This, though ... this is our home.

AL: It's big.

HENRY: Room for the kids.

AL: That's great. *(Henry gently shuts the door that connects the living room to the bedroom hallway.)*

HENRY: *(Softly.)* I ... actually I'm gonna go see somebody.

AL: Uh-huh.

HENRY: This is between us, right? Between friends.

AL: Of course.

HENRY: Next week. To a doctor.

AL: To see if you're firing blanks.

HENRY: No, but. Just to ... check things out. We got pregnant so easily a few years back. I don't know what's happening now.

AL: I'm sorry.

HENRY: Driving me crazy. Thinking about it. You know? Is it my fault? What kind of a, you know, man am I? To be a father, is '"

AL: Overrated.

HENRY: I was going to say, one of life's high honors.

AL: You would say that. Like that. I'd say overrated. But if it's what you want and you want to know ...

HENRY: I need to know.

AL: I support you in that, buddy.

HENRY: *(Wistful; takes his time.)* What happened to us ... a lot of couples, that ruins them. I was worried, but it happened just the opposite. Gina latched on to me, we were closer than ever. Now, it's just, I want to know about me.

AL: I'm behind you a hundred percent. *(Looks around.)* How are you - if you don't mind my asking - how are you set for money?

HENRY: We're okay. Things are tight. But we're okay. *(Pause.)* Actually about to rent out the upstairs room.

AL: Here?

HENRY: There's a back staircase, got its own door. *(Re: stairwell door.)* This locks off hom the inside, it's a private residence then. Bathroom. Small. For a grad student, somebody, they don't care. Little extra cash.

AL: It's a good idea.

HENRY: I made a mess up there, though. Room has an old fireplace, chimney. I was cleaning out the flue and screwed something up - filled the place with soot. Nearly choked to death.

AL: Yikes.

HENRY: Got it mostly cleaned up by now, should be ready to rent by next week. I haven't placed the ads yet, but someone'll grab it quick.

AL: I'm sure. *(Looks around.)* God, it feels good to be out of there ... *(Beat.)*

HENRY: Can I ask you something?

AL: Of Course.

HENRY: What were you talking about before ... about me not being free?

AL: Yes.

HENRY: What did you mean?

AL: What did I mean?

HENRY: That maybe I'm not free?

AL: Are you free?

HENRY: I still don't know what you mean by that. I'm my own boss, I have an income and I support my wife. I'm the man of a house. Well, right now it's an apartment, but ... *(Re: the model)* Soon it's going to be *this* house. I mean, I live in America. I vote. I'm not a criminal: I certainly *feel* free.

AL: Are you happy?

HENRY: Am I happy?

AL: Yes. When you really think about it ... are you satisfied?

HENRY: I don't know.

AL: Remember when I said I'd been talking to the crews on my
boats?

HENRY: Yes.

.AL: We talk about Ralph Waldo Emerson's ideas.

HENRY: Okay.

AL: He wrote an essay called "Self-Reliance." Have you read it?

HENRY: No. Maybe in high school.

AL: Look — *(Sharing an important secret.)* Before I went to Maine — for my first two years there, really — I was shackled by an incredible weight.

HENRY: Shackled? A weight?

AL: I was at war with my own body.

HENRY: I don't follow you.

AL: I wasn't fulfilled, satisfied, because I was lying to myself at the time I was dating this woman, Julie, but kept feeling this pull. ... away from her. Then I met Beth.

HENRY: A woman you're seeing now.

AL: She's incredible.

HENRY: Good for you.

AL: Which has made things between Julie and me better.

HENRY: *(Pause.)* Because you're seeing them both.

AL: But, Beth ... I swear to God ... she's married to this unbelievable loser. She and I make each other very happy.

HENRY: You shouldn't do that.

AL: Why not?

HENRY: If he's such a loser, why doesn't she leave him?

AL: Why should she *have* to? It's just a bunch of expensive, redtape headache anyway.

HENRY: You shouldn't.

AL: Can you tell me why?

HENRY: It's a good rule to follow. . .'

AL: I make my own rules. It's healthier. "Man is clapped into jail by his consciousness."

HENRY: Dating some married woman ... as well as another one at the same time, your rules allow for that?

AL: The rules allow for anything that completes a person. Don't you think it's exhausting to walk around lying to yourself about the things you want? My crews and I ... accross the board, everyone is happier, in better shape, more productive ... I know this sounds crazy, but our hauls are bigger and the company is making more money than ever. .

HENRY: You think that's because your men are screwmg around on their wives.

AL: First off: Not just men. I've got women on my boats and they've changed their lives, too. Same results.

HENRY: You're right: This does sound crazy.

AL: Do you cheat on Gina?

HENRY: Absolutely not.

AL: You think about it. .

HENRY: Everyone thinks about it. Still a good thing to avoid.

AL: What's her name?

HENRY: I don't want to talk about this.

AL: What's her name?

HENRY: I said I don't want to talk -

AL: You look at her, feels like you got your knees knocked out from under you. Can't breathe.

HENRY: Please drop it.

AL: I will if you tell me her name.

HENRY: *(Pause.)* Susan.

AL: That's a pretty name.

Reservoir
Eric Henry Sanders

Dramatic
Frank Hasek, 21
Staff Sergeant, 26

> *A young veteran, Private Frank Hasek, struggles to keep his job as a mechanic in order to support Marisa, the mother of his newborn son. However, unsettling visions and a series of unfortunate events threaten to upend his career and derail his relationship. Although he seeks help from an overworked psychiatrist at VA hospital, his behavior becomes increasingly erratic, and threatens to turn violent when he discovers that Marisa is having an affair with his Staff Sergeant. Here Hasek encounters his Staff Sergeant for the first time.*

> *The Staff Sergeant's office.*
> *Hasek is staring. His expression is completely blank as if he's catatonic. This goes on for too long. The Sergeant enters, holding some papers. He's clearly amused. Hasek doesn't notice him until after he's been spoken to.*

SERGEANT: I gotta hand it to you. Did you read this thing? I mean, did they send you a copy too? Because it's probably one of the funniest fucking things I've ever seen. Private?
(Hasek looks at him for the first time. He salutes.)
HASEK: Yes, Sir?
SERGEANT: I'm a sergeant.
HASEK: Yes, Sir.
SERGEANT: Only officers get saluted.
HASEK: *(Mumbles.)*
    Oh.
SERGEANT: You know that?
HASEK: Yes, Sir.
SERGEANT: How long have you been away?
HASEK: Fifteen months.
SERGEANT: Christ. Don't they teach you anything?
HASEK: I'm not sure how to answer that.
SERGEANT: I don't blame you –
HASEK: Thanks –

SERGEANT: It's not your fault, it's about whoever trained you.

HASEK: There were a couple different people.

SERGEANT: Your name's Ha-sick?

HASEK: Ha-shek.

SERGEANT: I've wanted to ask you: what kind of a name is that?

HASEK: I don't know. American?

SERGEANT: No. More like Polish or Czech.

HASEK: Is it?

SERGEANT: Do you know why you're here?

HASEK: Yes, Sir.

SERGEANT: You don't need -- I don't want you to keep calling me 'Sir.'
(Hasek nods.)
They want me to reprimand you.

HASEK: Are they going to discharge me?

SERGEANT: Did you want to get discharged?

HASEK: No --

SERGEANT: Is that why you -- ?

HASEK: -- I didn't --

SERGEANT: I guess the question is --

HASEK: -- They can't!

SERGEANT: Actually, yeah, they can.

HASEK: What would I say to Marisa?

SERGEANT: 'That your girl?

HASEK: What's she going to do if they discharge me?

SERGEANT: Maybe you should have considered that --

HASEK: She had a baby. We did. When I was in country.

SERGEANT: So you don't want to get kicked out?

HASEK: No, Sir.

SERGEANT: What were you doing then?

HASEK: Nothing.

SERGEANT: It wasn't "nothing" exactly --

HASEK: -- It -- I --

SERGEANT: -- You can't say it was "nothing."

HASEK: It's not what they said.

SERGEANT: I'm thinking maybe you admit doing what you did, and I'll figure out what to do about it.

HASEK: I didn't do anything.

SERGEANT: Did you read the letter they sent you?

HASEK: I don't have it with me.

SERGEANT: I was just wondering if you read it.

HASEK: I read it.

SERGEANT: And you're saying it's not true that you scratched your balls on national television?

HASEK: Not, Sir.

SERGEANT: Not true?

HASEK: Not true.

SERGEANT: Did they send you the video?

HASEK: I mean, I did what you said I did --

SERGEANT: I know you did.

HASEK: -- What they wrote in the, the, --

SERGEANT: The tape made that pretty clear.

HASEK: I did that, but I didn't know I was on national television.

SERGEANT: How's that?

HASEK: I didn't --

SERGEANT: Didn't you see the cameras?

HASEK: Yes. I mean --

SERGEANT: You knew you were at a press conference, right?

HASEK: What happened was --

SERGEANT: I hope you're not trying to tell me you're that stupid.

HASEK: What happened was they had us waiting for three hours. We were only supposed to be there for a little while, but there was a bomb scare or something, so the guy, the, the Congressman --

SERGEANT: -- Senator --

HASEK: -- was late. And they had us waiting with our gear because we were shipping back stateside.

SERGEANT: The report says you performed a "nut check."

HASEK: Yes, Sir.

SERGEANT: You read it?

HASEK: Yes.

SERGEANT: That doesn't sound like a casual scratch.

HASEK: I had an itch.

SERGEANT: They make it sound like there was deliberate provocation.

HASEK: It wasn't --I didn't know.

SERGEANT: It was a case of bad timing.

HASEK: It was hot. Everyone was hot. I had my gear --

SERGEANT: Yeah, you said that.

HASEK: -- but they kept us waiting.

SERGEANT: You had to scratch, and you didn't know you were on camera.

HASEK: Yes, Sir.

(Sergeant suppresses a laugh.)

SERGEANT: Did they ever get the press conference started?

HASEK: After three hours. We were the background.

SERGEANT: Uh, huh.

HASEK: It was bad timing, like you said.

SERGEANT: This is the first time I've read the phrase "nut check" in a US Army report.

HASEK: Sorry.

SERGEANT: I wish all my paperwork made me laugh like that.

HASEK: Do you think I'll be discharged?

SERGEANT: I'll put it down that it was a dumb stunt, but that you're sorry.

HASEK: It wasn't —

SERGEANT: That you admit you were in the wrong.

HASEK: It's just --

SERGEANT: And in the meantime, maybe you can do something for me.

HASEK: Like what?

SERGEANT: You know Ed Shultz? He said you designed a pretty cool tattoo for him.

HASEK: I worked at an ink shop a couple of summers.

SERGEANT: You think you could do that for me?

HASEK: I guess.

SERGEANT: I was thinking of something across my shoulders. A dragon or tiger or something.

HASEK: I only drew the stencil for Shultz. I didn't ink it.

SERGEANT: But you know how?

HASEK: It takes a long time to do it right.

SERGEANT: I've got time.

> *(Pause)*
>
> You think you could get hold of the right equipment?

HASEK: I'm not sure.

SERGEANT: Why don't you ask around? And, maybe you could make a couple of stencils, so I have something to choose from.

HASEK: You'll talk to them about the discharge?

SERGEANT: I can't promise anything.

HASEK: But you'll talk to them?

SERGEANT: Until then, try not scratch yourself on national television.

Still Life

Alexander Dinelaris

Seriocomic
Jeff, 30's. A trend analyst
Terry, 30's. His boss

> *With nowhere else to turn and an important pitch to be made, Terry turns to his star analyst to bail him out at the last minute. Jeff taps into his own frustrations to brilliantly sum up the feelings of an entire generation, and give his boss the perfect pitch.*

> *Jeff sits behind a desk. Terry, his boss and friend, stands in front of the desk and slams down a bucket of fried chicken.*

JEFF: What is that?
TERRY: Chicken
JEFF: Uh-huh.
TERRY: Fried chicken.
JEFF: I'm not hungry.
TERRY: OK.
    (The two men stand silently for a moment.)
JEFF: Terry?
TERRY: Help me.
JEFF: I have three hours to get this—
TERRY: Help me.
JEFF: Terry.
TERRY: Jeff.
JEFF: What?
TERRY: Help me. *(A Beat.)* I love you. *(A Beat.)* Help.
    (Jeff puts aside what he was working on.)
JEFF: Let's hear it.
TERRY: Okay. Here we go. Southern-- You rock, by the way. Southern Fried Chicken. We gotta present tomorrow.
JEFF: Tomorrow?
TERRY: That's right.
JEFF: What do you have so far?
TERRY: What do you mean?
JEFF: What do you have?

(A Beat.)

TERRY: *(pointing to the bucket)*
 Chicken.

JEFF: Come on...

TERRY: Help me. Your dick is huge. Help me.

JEFF: Adam had three months to put together a—

TERRY: Adam's fucked.

JEFF: What do you mean?

TERRY: His wife left him. His mind hasn't exactly been—

JEFF: His wife left him?

TERRY: Yeah. Took the kids. Took the loot, and cut out with one of the New Jersey Nets. Adam's fucked.

JEFF: I'm just saying, he did all the research on this, he should—

TERRY: Adam's a douche bag. You're a god. Chicken. Go.

JEFF: You don't have anything?

TERRY: No. Yeah. I have new packaging. Fancy containers. Steamed veggie sides. A salad menu. I have "get away from greasy buckets". Cultural trends. Health awareness. Sushi nation. Reposition, repackage, blah, blah, blah. I've heard it before. It sucks. What do you got?

JEFF: That's what Adam came up with?

TERRY: Adam blows poodles, Jeffrey. What do you have? I need something I can sell here. Bottom of the ninth, two outs. I'm going to the bullpen. Give it to me.

JEFF: I don't know. I haven't had time to—

TERRY: I'll take what you give me.

JEFF: *(staring at the bucket)*
 Okay, hang on...

TERRY: I'm hanging. I'm hanging. I'm hung. Not like you, you stud, but—

JEFF: Terry—

TERRY: Right. Sorry. Take your time.
 (Terry watches as Jeff continues to stare. Jeff gets up and circles the desk, looking for it. Finally, he stops pacing.)
 What? Give it to me.

JEFF: Go the other way.

TERRY: Good. Fuck. I like it. What do you mean?

JEFF: Don't run away from it. Run back to it.

TERRY: Run back to it. Listen to you. You're a fucking-- You're like-- FUCK/ What's the angle?

JEFF: We're all tired...

TERRY: Sure we're tired. Shit, I'm tired, right now.

JEFF: We're tired of being afraid...

TERRY: ...I'm listening...

JEFF: ...Afraid to live. Hole in the ozone. Lead in our tap water. Watch our carbs. Watch our kids. We're grown men, throwing around cholesterol numbers like we used to throw around bowling scores. We're pissed off. Why shouldn't we be? Every day someone else reminds us that if we don't watch out, we're gonna lose six years off our lives. And deep down, we're thinking, "What six years? Seventy-eight to eighty-four?" We just want to live. Right now. Today. We go out of our way to be careful and then we watch the news and find out that sixteen people just bought it because some bus driver washed his Paxil down with Jack Daniels, took his bus and made a drive through out of a shoe store. Well, great. Lotta good the bran muffin and the Lipitor did them. *(A Beat.)* We want to live. More than that, we want to enjoy living. You know what else we want?

TERRY: Chicken?

JEFF: Fried chicken.

TERRY: Fuckin' A.

(Terry grabs a piece of chicken.)

JEFF: Run back to it. Anchor it in the mind of the consumer. "Remember when you lost that little league game? Your seventh grade boyfriend broke up with you? The baking soda and vinegar volcano you made for Earth science only got you a C? *(A Beat.)* Where'd your mom take you?"

TERRY: *(Mouth full.)*
Southern Fried Chicken.

JEFF: Southern Fried Chicken. Comfort food. Nostalgia. *(Sincerely.)* "You weren't scared then. Don't be scared now. Eat your chicken".

TERRY: I am. It's good.

JEFF: Adam wants to change the package? He might be wrong.

TERRY: He might be an asshole!

JEFF: *(pointing to the bucket)*
Look at that. It's timeless. An American classic. You're gonna fuck with that? Why? You're worried about a few grease stains on the bucket? Hey. Grease stains are how you know it's good. *(A Beat.)* We're afraid and we're pissed off. "Pleasure Revenge". That's the angle.

TERRY: See? That's why I hired you. You're my closer.

JEFF: Hey. Take it easy on Adam. He's a good guy, he just took an elbow.

TERRY: You hardly know him.

JEFF: He's a good guy. Go easy.

TERRY: You're a big pussy, you know that?

JEFF: Yeah.

TERRY: I won't hold it against you.

(Terry heads for the door. He turns back.)

You know what? There's a thing tonight, down in the village. I want you to come.

JEFF: No. *(A Beat.)* What is it?

TERRY: I don't know. A photo exhibit or something. Some hot new photographer. Eastman is sponsoring. All the brass is gonna be there.

JEFF: A photo exhibit?

TERRY: Who cares? Hot chicks in cocktail dresses getting bombed on champagne. It'll be a buffet.

JEFF: I can't go.

TERRY: You're gonna go. I'll have Nina e-mail you the info.

JEFF: Fine. *(A Beat.)* Don't forget your chicken.

(Terry crosses back to get the chicken.)

TERRY: Pleasure Revenge.

JEFF: Pleasure Revenge. We all want to live. We just need permission. Cause we already know the truth.

TERRY: Sure we do. *(A Beat.)* What's the truth?

JEFF: We're all going to die.

Trust

Paul Weitz

Comic
Harry, late-20s
Morton, probably early 30s

Harry, a newly minted dot-com millionaire, has recently visited an S & M dungeon. To his surprise, his dominatrix turns out to be a woman he went to high school with named Prudence. Morton is a shady character who is Prudence's boyfriend. He think he might be able to blackmail Harry into making a contribution for his foundation (which may or not exist), which supposedly tries to help sex workers transition into another line of work.

(Lights up on Harry's office. Retro-modern furniture. Harry lets Morton into his office.)

MORTON: Hi. Morton Melville Cohen.

(they shake hands)

Nice office.

HARRY: Thanks.

MORTON: I thought it would be bigger.

HARRY: Oh. Well, it's big enough for me. Have a seat. Want some water?

MORTON: Your secretary gave me some already.

(holds up a bottled water)

Fiji water. What do you want to bet there's a whole lot of Fijians walking around thirsty going hey, where's all the fucking water?

HARRY: It's possible.

MORTON: Cause we're drinking all their water...Do you drink a lot of water? I can't, it makes me urinate. I mean, our bodies are ninety percent water, right? The rest is what, meat?

HARRY: Yeah...uh...

MORTON: Bone. Gristle. The soul. You think the soul exists?

HARRY: I uh, I don't know. Haven't really been...pondering that too much.

MORTON: What else is there to ponder?

HARRY: ...Okay, yeah, I believe the soul exists. I'll go out on a limb.

MORTON: I like it. I like it.

HARRY: I don't have any inside information or anything, don't get too excited. Umm, so... You're a friend of Prudence's?

MORTON: Yeah. I'm sort of her best friend. I'm sort of her husband.

HARRY: She didn't mention she's married.

MORTON: She's not. I said I was "sort of" her husband...So it's terrific that you have this charitable foundation. It's great that you're giving back.

HARRY: It's fun for me, yes.

MORTON: Must be fun for you. You must feel like Santa Claus. Bigger. Like Santa Claus with a hard-on, right?

HARRY: *(Pause.)*

Sure.

MORTON: Santa Claus with a nuclear bomb. A nuclear bomb for a phallus.

HARRY: Umm –

MORTON: Anyway, Prudence told me your foundation gives grants to nonprofit organizations.

HARRY: Yes. We do.

MORTON: Which was exciting to me because I happen to have a nonprofit organization.

HARRY: ...That's great. What is it?

MORTON: It's called "A Second Pants."

HARRY: "A Second Pants."

MORTON: Yeah. It's a play on words.

HARRY: And what does "A Second Pants" do?

MORTON: "A Second Pants" helps workers in the sex-industry to reenter the normal working world. It helps them conquer their addiction to the degrading, disgusting world of sex for hire.

HARRY: It sounds like a good idea.

MORTON: You think so?

HARRY: Absolutely.

MORTON: I myself have a little ambivalence about it. Because a good slut is hard to find. Am I right?

HARRY: *(Pause.)*

...Why don't you send over a prospectus for your

organization, and I'll pass it on to the board of directors.

MORTON: Actually, I'm still working on the prospectus.

HARRY: When it's done, send it over.

MORTON: The thing is, I have writer's block. I'm better at oral exams. I like telling people things. For instance I wouldn't mind telling your wife that you go to S and M parlors to have your ass spanked and your nipples twisted.

HARRY: ...I didn't --

MORTON: Oh come on. I know all about it. I have nothing against it. I just happen to be a pitcher, not a catcher. No big deal to me. Of course other people, notably spouses, tend to get a little freaked out by it. They don't like to imagine their big strong husband with his ass in the air, just getting wailed on, shouting "Mommy! Mommy! Spank me!"

HARRY: What do you want?

MORTON: What I want is to crack your skull open.

HARRY: I'm calling the police.

MORTON: Go ahead. Then I'll call your wife. I have your home number.

(*Pause.*)

Don't take it personally, I don't want to crack open your skull in particular. I don't like any of her clients. I guess I'm jealous. Crazy, huh? I mean you're really just a bunch of queers who are too afraid to take it up the ass, so you pay a woman to piss and shit on you. Am I right?

HARRY: I'm sure you know more about it than I do.

MORTON: I know more about a lot of things than you do.

HARRY: You're a pretty insecure person, aren't you?

MORTON: Insecure?

HARRY: You give that impression.

MORTON: What are you, fucking with me? You're not the fucker here, you're the fuckee. You're the one in trouble, because you're the pervert. (*Pause.*) So what I want is a thirty-thousand dollar deposit for my foundation. That's nothing for you. You blow your nose in that kind of money.

HARRY: But it's a hell of a lot to you.

MORTON: Yeah. I could pay off a debt with it.

(*Pause.*)

I want the money by Monday. Or else I bring the hammer down.

(*Harry laughs*)

What are you laughing at?

HARRY: Sorry.

MORTON: Are you laughing at me?

HARRY: No. Just...your expressions.

MORTON: What about them?

HARRY: It's like you saw them in a movie.

(*Morton grabs Harry's neck.*)

MORTON: Do you want to die?

HARRY: -- No --

MORTON: Have you seen this in a movie?

HARRY: Let go --

MORTON: Have you seen someone choking the snot out of you in a movie?

(*Harry pries Morton's fingers off his throat. He coughs.*)

MORTON: Sorry. You alright? Here, have some water.

(He holds out his water.)
HARRY: That's okay.
(Harry drinks from his own water.)
MORTON: You made me do that. I'm just a businessman.
HARRY: Yeah...everyone is.
(Harry feels his throat.)
MORTON: Alright, then. Monday. Money. Or else. Don't make me fuck your life, Harry. Because I'll do it. I will hold your life down and fuck it.

Zorro X 2

Bernardo Solano

Comic
Diego, 20s
Eddie, 30s-40s

> *Diego is a self-confessed computer geek who has recently begun teaching computer science at a wealthy private school in the Southwest. He's had some bad breaks in his life and is somewhat emotionally scarred and easily intimidated. Eddie is an older man who claims he is the masked hero Zorro, and that he has taken the job of school custodian in order to cloak his true identity. Eddie suffers from vivid nightmares in which he does battle with the villain "El Monstruo," a nightmare which always ends badly. Eddie and Diego have recently met and Diego doesn't quite know what to make of this man who believes he is a fictional character from movies and television. In this scene, Diego has just embarrassed himself in front of an attractive female teacher, but not to worry, Eddie sees something in Diego he's not yet able to see himself.*

DIEGO: Why'd I do that?

EDDIE: Because it's what Zorro would do.

DIEGO: I don't get it.

EDDIE: Oye. If you'd done your homework you'd know that if Zorro acted like Zorro in his daily life, everyone would know his identity. The forces of oppression and injustice would find him in an instant, incarcerate him, torture him, and in so doing, prevent him from undermining their nefarious plots to rule the world. And more importantly, prevent him from inspiring the oppressed. You see, as long as Zorro remains free, the people can imagine the day that they too will be free. Thus they are inspired to work toward realizing that elusive yet oh-so-real goal because one man ...Zorro ... is among them, leaving his mark for all to see. *(He slowly walks around Diego.)* Mira. A few minutes ago you could barely balance your body over your feet. Your heart mumbled. Your dreams stuck in the muck of mediocrity. But now. You stand taller. Your feet are firmly planted. Your heart sings. Your dreams float toward the firmament. *(Beat.)* It is good you let me see this side of you.

DIEGO: You see all this ...in me?

EDDIE: I do.

DIEGO: How?

EDDIE: Because I am Zorro. And Zorro can see things other men can't. Now, let us speak of your other self ...

DIEGO: The one people ridicule?

EDDIE: Why do you say that?

DIEGO: I'm a geek. I know that. I've always known it.

EDDIE: Define geek.

DIEGO: Geek is a guy who knows a lot about something. Math, Science, nano-technology-whatever everyone else could care less about. When other kids were worrying about who's seen with who, who takes who to the prom ... I was writing computer code. Whenever the bullies were bored, they'd come looking for me for a little entertainment. Ever heard of that movie, "Carrie?"

EDDIE: *(Rapid fire)* Stephen King novel, directed by Brian de Palma, starring Sissy Spacek. At the homecoming dance, bucket of pig's blood dumped on Carrie's head, Carrie kills the whole school.

DIEGO: Yeah, I guess you have heard of it. Anyway, I'm Carrie, except it wasn't pig's blood and I didn't kill the whole school. I just disappeared the day after graduation. *(Beat.)* I was "less than" and that's all they needed to know.

EDDIE: You were different. Different scares people, and that makes them do stupid things. Anyway, you shouldn't resent that part of yourself. You must love it. And then use it. It is the cloak that shields you from prying eyes.

DIEGO: What about you? Don't you have ...a "cloak"?

EDDIE: Of course I do. They think I'm addled. The town idiot. A buffoon. A man who talks to himself. A man who sees things that other men can't.

DIEGO: Okay, maybe you're not exactly who I thought you were.

(A crashing sound from outside. Eddie reacts by taking cover in an almost feral way.)

EDDIE: Take cover!

DIEGO: I think it was just somebody dropping something outside.

EDDIE: No! It was him!

DIEGO: No, it was just-

EDDIE: El Monstruo!

DIEGO: The Monster?

EDDIE: Hide me, please, hide me!

DIEGO: There's nothing out there, Eddie.

EDDIE: You don't understand! He's found me! I've been hiding a long time, playing like I'm crazy, fooling everybody, thinking he'd never look for me

in all those places!

DIEGO: Eddie, there's nobody out there except for some workers.

(Eddie is on his hands and knees-he seems to be losing whatever grip on reality he had.)

EDDIE: No lo oyes?! He's out there!! And he found me because of you! Because I came out of hiding for you! This is what I get for trying to help!

DIEGO: I'm going for help-

EDDIE: No, don't leave me!

DIEGO: Okay, okay.

(Eddie grabs and holds on to Diego for dear life.)

EDDIE: He's dead! He's dead because of me!

DIEGO: Who-El Monstruo?

EDDIE: No! The guy! The guy! El Inocente! I killed him!

DIEGO: It's okay, Eddie. You're here now. With me. You're here.

EDDIE: Don't let go. Don't let go. Don't let go.

(This time, directly to Diego) Don't let go.

Rights and permissions

The entire text of each play may be obtained by contacting the rights holder.

Note: For playwrights whose names are followed by an asterisk (*), information can be found about them on the "Meet our authors" web page at www.smithandkraus.com

MONOLOGUES

ABSALOM © 2010 by Zoe Kazan. Reprinted by permission of Zoe Kazan. For performance rights, contact Dramatists Play Service, 440 Park Ave. S., New York, NY 10016 (www.dramatists. com) (212-683-8960).

ALIVE AND WELL © 2009 by Kenny Finkle. Reprinted by permission of Beth Blickers, Abrams Artists Agency. For performance rights, contact Beth Blickers (beth.blickers@abramsartny.com).

BACHELORETTE © 2008 by Leslye Headland. Reprinted by permission of Bruce Ostler, Bret Adams Ltd. For performance rights, contact Dramatists Play Service, 440 Park Ave. S, New York, NY 10016 (www.dramatists.com) (212-683-8960).

BARBARY FOX © 2009 by Don Nigro. Reprinted by permission of Don Nigro. For performance rights, contact Samuel French, Inc. (www.samuelfrench.com) (212-206-8990).

BASS FOR PICASSO © 2010 by Kate Moira Ryan. Reprinted by permission of Beth Blickers, Abrams Artists Agency. For performance rights, contact Beth Blickers (beth.blickers@ abramsartny.com).

BOTTOM OF THE WORLD © 2010 by Lucy Thurber. Reprinted by permission of Beth Blickers, Abrams Artists Agency. For performance rights, contact Dramatists Play Service, 440 Park Ave. S., New York, NY 10016 (www.dramatists.com) (212-683-8960).

A BRIGHT NEW BOISE © 2010 by Samuel D. Hunter.* Reprinted by permission of Derek Zasky, William Morris Endeavor Entertainment. For performance rights, contact Samuel French, Inc. (www.samuelfrench.com) (212-206-8990)

CHING CHONG CHINAMAN © 2008 by Lauren Yee. Reprinted by permission of Lauren Yee. For performance rights, contact Lauren Yee (lauren.d.yee@gmail.com).

COLLAPSE © 2010 by Allison Moore. Reprinted by permission of Beth Blickers   Maura Teitelbaum, Abrams Artists Agency. For performance rights, contact Beth Blickers (beth. blickers@abramsartny.com) or Maura Teitelbaum (maura.teitelbaum@abramsartnyc.com)

A COMMON VISION © 2009 by Neena Beber. Reprinted by permission of Mark Subias, Subias Agency. For performance rights, contact Samuel French, Inc. (www.samuelfrench.com) (212-206-8990).

A CONFLUENCE OF DREAMING © 2010 by Tammy Ryan.* Reprinted by permission of Susan Gurman, Susan Gurman Agency. For performance rights, contact Broadway Play Publishing, 56 E. 81st St., New York, NY 10021 (www.broadwayplaypubl.com) (212-772-8334.)

CRAZY HORSE AND THREE STARS © 2010 by David Wiltse.* Reprinted by permission of David Wiltse. For performance rights, contact Broadway Play Publishing, 56 E. 81st St., New York, NY 10021 (www.broadwayplaypubl.com) 212-772-8334.

THE DIVINE SISTER © 2010 by Charles Busch.* Reprinted by permission of Olivier Sultan, Creative Artists Agency. For performance rights, contact Samuel French, Inc. (www.samuelfrench. com) (212-206-8990).

DUSK RINGS A BELL © 2010 by Stephen Belber. Reprinted by permission of Stephen Belber. For performance rights, contact Dramatists Play Service, 440 Park Ave. S., New York, NY 10016 (www.dramatists.com) (212-683-8960).

EASTER MONDAY © 2009 by Hal Corley.* Reprinted by permission of Barbara Hogenson, Barbara Hogenson Agency. For performance rights, contact Samuel French, Inc. (www. samuelfrench.com) (212-206-8990).

EXTINCTION © 2010 by Gabe McKinley.* Reprinted by permission of Ron Gwiazda, Abrams Artists Agency. For performance rights, contact Samuel French, Inc. (www.samuelfrench.com) (212-206-8990).

A FELLOW OF INFINITE JEST © 2010 by Don Nigro. Reprinted by permission of Don Nigro. For performance rights, contact Samuel French, Inc. (www.samuelfrench.com) (212-206-8990).

GEOMETRY OF FIRE © 2010 by Stephen Belber. Reprinted by permission of Stephen Belber. For performance rights, contact Dramatists Play Service, 440 Park Ave. S., New York, NY 10016 (www.dramatists.com) (212-683-8960).

GOLDFISH © 2010 by John Kolvenbach.* Reprinted by permission of Chris Till, Creative Artists Agency. For performance rights, contact Dramatists Play Service, 440 Park Ave. S., New York, NY 10016 (www.dramatists.com) (212-683-8960).

GRAND CAYMAN © 2009 by Don Nigro. Reprinted by permission of Don Nigro. For performance rights, contact Samuel French, Inc. (www.samuelfrench.com) (212-206-8990).

GRUESOME PLAYGROUND INJURIES © 2011 by Rajiv Joseph.* Reprinted by permission of Seth Glewen, The Gersh Agency. For performance rights, contact Dramatists Play Service, 440 Park Ave. S., New York, NY 10016 (www.dramatists.com) (212-683-8960).

HELLO HERMAN © 2010 by John Buffalo Mailer.* Reprinted by permission of John Buffalo Mailer. For performance rights, contact Dramatists Play Service, 440 Park Ave. S, New York, NY 10016 (www.dramatists.com) (212-683-8960).

IN GOD'S HAT © 2010 by Richard Taylor.* Reprinted by permission of Derek Zasky, William Morris Endeavor Entertainment. For performance rights, contact Derek Zasky (dsz@ wmeentertainment.com)

THE IRISH CURSE © 2005 by Martin Casella.* Reprinted by permission of Elaine Devlin, Elaine Devlin Literary, Inc. For performance rights, contact Samuel French, Inc. (www. samuelfrench.com) (212-206-8990).

THE LANGUAGE ARCHIVE © 2010 by Julia Cho.* Reprinted by permission of John

Buzzetti, William Morris Endeavor Entertainment. For performance rights, contact Dramatists Play Service, 440 Park Ave. S., New York, NY 10016 (www.dramatists.com) (212-683-8960).

THE LANGUAGE OF TREES © 2010 by Steven Levenson.* Reprinted by permission of Chris Till, Creative Artists Agency. For performance rights, contact Dramatists Play Service, 440 Park Ave. S., New York, NY 10016 (www.dramatists.com) (212-683-8960).

LASCIVIOUS SOMETHING © 2011 by Savage Candy Productions f/s/o Sheila Callaghan * c/o The Gersh Agency. Reprinted by permission of Seth Glewen The Gersh Agency. For performance rights, contact Samuel French, Inc. (www.samuelfrench.com) (212-206-8990)

LOCAL NOBODY © 2009 by Nicole Pandolfo.* Reprinted by permission of Nicole Pandolfo. For performance rights, contact Nicole Pandolfo (nicole.e.pandolfo@gmail.com).

THE LONG RED ROAD © 2010 by Brett C. Leonard.* Reprinted by permission of Brett C. Leonard. For performance rights, contact Broadway Play Publishing, 56 E. 81st St., New York, NY 10021 (www.broadwayplaypubl.com) 212-772-8334.

LOVE TOWN © 2010 by Michael Kaplan. Reprinted by permission of Michael Kaplan. For performance rights, contact Samuel French, Inc. (www.samuelfrench.com) (212-206-8990).

MATTHEW AND THE PASTOR'S WIFE © 2010 by Robert Askins. Reprinted by permission of Robert Askins. For performance rights, contact Robert Askins (rfa2000@gmail.com).

MOTHERHOUSE © 2010 by Victor Lodato. Reprinted by permission of Beth Blickers & Morgan Jenness, Abrams Artists Agency. For performance rights, contact Samuel French, Inc. (www.samuelfrench.com) (212-206-8990).

OFFICE HOURS © 2010 by A. R. Gurney.* Reprinted by permission of Jonathan Lomma, William Morris Endeavor Entertainment. For performance rights, contact Broadway Play Publishing, 56 E. 81st St., New York, NY 10021 (www.broadwayplaypubl.com) 212-772-8334.

PIGMALION © 2008 by Mark Dunn.* Reprinted by permission of Mark Dunn. For performance rights, contact Samuel French, Inc. (www.samuelfrench.com) (212-206-8990).

THE RANT © 2010 by Andrew Case.* Reprinted by permission of Ron Gwiazda, Abrams Artists Agency. For performance rights, contact Dramatists Play Service, 440 Park Ave. S., New York, NY 10016 (www.dramatists.com) (212-683-8960).

RANTOUL AND DIE © 2010 by Mark Roberts. Reprinted by permission of Chris Till, Creative Artists Agency. For performance rights, contact Dramatists Play Service, 440 Park Ave. S., New York, NY 10016 (www.dramatists.com) (212-683-8960).

A RUSSIAN PLAY © 2004, 2005 by Don Nigro. Reprinted by permission of Don Nigro. For performance rights, contact Samuel French, Inc. (www.samuelfrench.com) (212-206-8990).

SEVEN MINUTES IN HEAVEN © 2010 by Steven Levenson.* Reprinted by permission of Chris Till, Creative Artists Agency. For performance rights, contact Playscripts, Inc., 450 7th Ave. #803, New York, NY 10123. www.playscripts.com (phone 866-NEWPLAY).

STILL LIFE © 2009 by Alexander Dinelaris.* Reprinted by permission of Olivier Sultan, Creative Artists Agency. For performance rights, contact D.P.S.

THEY FLOAT UP © 2010 by Jacqueline Reingold. Reprinted by permission of Jacqueline Reingold. For performance rights, contact Mark Subias, Subias Agency (mark@marksubias.com).

THINGS OF DRY HOURS © 2010 by Naomi Wallace. Reprinted by permission of Ron Gwiazda, Abrams Artists Agency. For performance rights, contact Broadway Play Publishing, 56 E. 81st St., New York, NY 10021 (www.broadwayplaypubl.com) 212-772-8334.

THIS © 2010 by Melissa James Gibson. Reprinted by permission of Tiffany Mischeshin, Theatre Communications Group. For performance rights, contact Dramatists Play Service, 440 Park Ave. S., New York, NY 10016 (www.dramatists.com) (212-683-8960).

TIGERS BE STILL © 2010 by Kim Rosenstock.* Reprinted by permission of Derek Zasky, William Morris Endeavor Entertainment. For performance rights, contact Derek Zasky (dsz@wmeentertainment.com)

TIME STANDS STILL © 2010 by Donald Margulies. Reprinted by permission of Tiffany Mischeshin, Theatre Communications Group. For performance rights, contact Dramatists Play Service, 440 Park Ave. S., New York, NY 10016 (www.dramatists.com) (212-683-8960).

TRUST © 2010 by Paul Weitz.* Reprinted by permission of John Buzzetti, William Morris Endeavor Entertainment. For performance rights, contact Dramatists Play Service, 440 Park Ave. S., New York, NY 10016 (www.dramatists.com) (212-683-8960).

THE TYRANNY OF CLARITY © 2010 by Brian Dykstra. Reprinted by permission of Brian Dykstra. For performance rights, contact Brian Dykstra (briandykstra@earthlink.net).

WE ARE HERE © 2010 by Tracy Thorne.* Reprinted by permission of Peter Hagan, Abrams Artists Agency. For performance rights, contact Peter Hagan (peter.hagan@abramsartny.com).

SCENES

A BRIGHT NEW BOISE © 2010 by Samuel D. Hunter.* Reprinted by permission of Derek Zasky, William Morris Endeavor Entertainment. For performance rights, contact Samuel French, Inc. (www.samuelfrench.com) (212-206-8990)

DARKPOOL © 2010 by Don Nigro. Reprinted by permission of Don Nigro. For performance rights, contact Samuel French, Inc. (www.samuelfrench.com) (212-206-8990).

THE DEW POINT © 2009 by Neena Beber.* Reprinted by permission of Mark Subias, Subias Agency. For performance rights, contact Samuel French, Inc. (www.samuelfrench.com) (212-206-8990).

EXTINCTION © 2010 by Gabe McKinley.* Reprinted by permission of Ron Gwiazda, Abrams Artists Agency. For performance rights, contact Samuel French, Inc. (www.samuelfrench.com) (212-206-8990).

GIZMO LOVE © 2010 by John Kolvenbach.* Reprinted by permission of Chris Till, Creative Artists Agency. For performance rights, contact Dramatists Play Service, 440 Park Ave. S., New

York, NY 10016 (www.dramatists.com) (212-683-8960).

JAILBAIT © 2010 by Deirdre O'Connor. Reprinted by permission of Jessica Amato, The Gersh Agency. For performance rights, contact Dramatists Play Service, 440 Park Ave. S., New York, NY 10016 (www.dramatists.com) (212-683-8960).

THE LONG RED ROAD © 2010 by Brett C. Leonard.* Reprinted by permission of Brett C. Leonard. For performance rights, contact Broadway Play Publishing, 56 E. 81st St., New York, NY 10021 (www.broadwayplaypubl.com) 212-772-8334.

THE MAN WHO ATE MICHAEL ROCKEFELLER © 2010 by Jeff Cohen * . Reprinted by permission of Jeff Cohen. For performance rights, contact Jeff Cohen (cohenworthstreet@aol. com)

OFFICE HOURS © 2010 by A. R. Gurney.* Reprinted by permission of Jonathan Lomma, William Morris Endeavor Entertainment. For performance rights, contact Broadway Play Publishing, 56 E. 81st St., New York, NY 10021 (www.broadwayplaypubl.com) 212-772-8334.

RADIO FREE EMERSON © 2010 by Paul Grellong.* Reprinted by permission of Chris Till, Creative Artists Agency. For performance rights, contact Dramatists Play Service, 440 Park Ave. S., New York, NY 10016 (www.dramatists.com) (212-683-8960).

RESERVOIR © 2010 by Eric Henry Sanders. Reprinted by permission of Eric Henry Sanders. For performance rights, contact Eric Henry Sanders (esanders@hampshire.edu).

STILL LIFE © 2010 by Alexander Dinaris.* Reprinted by permission of Olivier Sultan, Creative Artists Agency. For performance rights, contact Dramatists Play Service, 440 Park Ave. S., New York, NY 10016 (www.dramatists.com) (212-683-8960).

TRUST © 2010 by Paul Weitz. Reprinted by permission of John Buzzetti, William Morris Endeavor Entertainment. For performance rights, contact Dramatists Play Service, 440 Park Ave. S., New York, NY 10016 (www.dramatists.com) (212-683-8960).

ZORRO X 2 © 2007 by Zorro Productions, Inc., ZORRO® and Bernardo Solano. Reprinted by permission of Bernard Solano. For performance rights, contact Broadway Play Publishing, 56 E. 81st St., New York, NY 10021 (www.broadwayplaypubl.com) 212-772-8334.